Environmental Policy for Business

Environmental Policy for Business

A Manager's Guide to Smart Regulation

Martin Perry

BUSINESS EXPERT PRESS

Environmental Policy for Business: A Manager's Guide to Smart Regulation
Copyright © Business Expert Press, LLC, 2015.

First published in 2015 by
Business Expert Press, LLC
222 East 46th Street, New York, NY 10017
www.businessexpertpress.com

ISBN-13: 978-1-60649-670-1 (paperback)
ISBN-13: 978-1-60649-671-8 (e-book)

Business Expert Press Principles for Responsible Management Education
Collection

Collection ISSN: 2331-0014 (print)
Collection ISSN: 2331-0022 (electronic)

Cover and interior design by S4Carlisle Publishing Services Private Ltd.,
Chennai, India

First edition: 2015

10 9 8 7 6 5 4 3 2 1

Printed in the United States of America.

Abstract

In the context of the worldwide concern with the sustainability of current forms of development, business managers are being required to engage with environmental policy more creatively than in the past. At the broadest level, business managers are being advised to embrace regulation as a source of competitive advantage rather than viewing it simply as a compliance cost and administrative burden. Irrespective of whether managers accept that "going beyond compliance" is a stimulus for innovation, business managers frequently face a policy environment in which choices need to be made over how policy agendas should be responded to. Contemporary policy approaches may mandate demonstration of best practice, without defining what constitutes best practice or use policy approaches that give the option of "paying for pollution" or investing in clean technology. Frequently, the argument is made that there are reputational gains to being a first mover and putting the organization ahead of regulation, but the implication can be considerable upfront investment for uncertain returns. Against this context, this book provides a guide to the new world of environmental regulation for managers within business and students with a particular interest in understanding how environmental regulation works.

The book commences by examining the argument that business self-interest justifies investment in initiatives to make business more environmentally sustainable than it was. It is frequently argued that actions for sustainability can be justified by a business case in which returns to the individual business outweigh the costs. Evidence that environmental conditions are tending to worsen while voluntary commitment appears to be growing casts doubts over the importance of environmental actions informed by a business case. Self-regulation has potential to go beyond purely voluntary action by individual enterprises, but effective self-regulation tends to require a high degree of industry cohesion and a willingness to include external parties in the design of schemes and monitoring of compliance. Ultimately, this book argues that government regulation is a necessary aspect of securing the transition to a more sustainable economy. The question then addressed is whether there is a smarter way to design environmental regulation than it has been in the past. Advocates of smart regulation see the potential for advancing the transition to environmental sustainability by designing regulation in ways that maximize the incentive on business to comply while raising the ambition of public policy.

The potential for smart environmental regulation is illustrated in the case of Japan's Top Runner Program. Chapter 2 goes on to examine the wider prospects for smart regulation by examining the main options for designing regulation. This includes summaries of responsive regulation, risk-based regulation, principle-based regulation, metaregulation, and market-based approaches. Prospects for these approaches to offer an alternative to command and control the traditional and most criticized form of regulation are examined. Two forms of regulation are then examined in detail: information sharing and emission trading. Both these regulatory designs have been advocated as superior ways of implementing environmental regulation, but where experience has shown that the theoretical advantages are hard to realize in practice. Chapter 5 considers a normative and a political interpretation of how environmental policy choices are made and argues that both point against seeking to promote a single best way to design regulation. Six principles of smart environmental regulation are outlined, which place the emphasis on using a combination of approaches customized to the environmental issue being addressed. The final chapter considers the implications of the doubts raised about smart regulation and discusses the messages for managers of organizations that aspire to be responsible and play a role in creating an environmentally sustainable world.

Key Words

Environment policy, sustainability, regulation, smart regulation, policy choices, self-regulation, business case, command and control, responsive regulation, risk-based regulation, principle-based regulation, market-based instruments, information sharing, emission trading, offsets.

Contents

Preface

This book came about from my teaching of business and sustainability to postgraduate students at Massey University. A great deal of the emphasis in business school teaching is on the advantages that business can obtain for themselves by improving their environmental performance and by being recognized as a responsible company. This claim generates a great deal of discussion but tends not to stand up to close scrutiny once a distinction between ecoefficiency and ecoeffectiveness is introduced. As attention shifts from merely examining whether business performance improves when investing in sustainability to an examination of what type of improvement is needed to bring a net gain for the environment, the importance of voluntary action tends to reduce. This opens up awareness of the need for regulation to push companies to take bigger steps toward a more sustainable pattern of economic development. This agenda has not been absent from business school teaching. There is a well-known claim that business has nothing to fear from regulation and that by demanding action be taken businesses can acquire a competitive advantage over companies operating in places with weak regulation. A gap in this argument is precisely what form of regulation will secure this virtuous outcome and how clear is the evidence that the regulation is effective in producing the double dividend of a better environment and more competitive business community. Much of the discussion about "smart" environmental regulation has been driven by a belief that market-based regulation works better for everyone than the traditional approach to regulation of command and control. This book is about this claim. It hopes to make managers and aspiring mangers more aware of the strengths and weakness of alternative ways of designing regulation and through this gain a greater appreciation of the role that regulation can play in creating a more sustainable world.

Martin Perry
Wellington, New Zealand
April 2015

CHAPTER 1

Environmental Policy: Government and Business Agendas

In the broadest sense, *policy* can be thought of as the set of principles and intentions used to guide decision making.[1] This is a useful interpretation as it draws attention to the way people as well as organizations make policy-informed decisions and how policy exists when action is not taken as well as when positive decisions to change behavior are taken. Nonetheless, this book focuses on perhaps a more generally understood interpretation of policy: initiatives designed by government agencies intending to achieve specific ends through efforts enshrined in *public policy* programs. These deliberate efforts are by and large responses to issues that are deemed sufficiently serious to justify efforts to curb individual and organizational behaviors that would occur otherwise in the absence of the policy intervention, typically with goals and objectives to be achieved over a specified time frame. Environmental policy as discussed in this book is concerned with the principles and intentions of policy programs that aim to protect and enhance the state of the physical environment and natural ecosystems. This encompasses a wide range of concerns, including the designation of national parks, wildlife protection, standards governing air and water quality, and the controls placed on individual land users. The particular interest is in environmental policy as it affects the contemporary concern with sustainability and that is directly concerned with engineering changes in business behavior.

Sustainability is the idea that today's population should limit its use of resources to that which at least ensures that future populations inherit a world of no lesser quality and environmental abundance.[2] Sustainability has modified the scope of environmental policy in at least three ways. First, it has broadened the issues to which policy is applied by increasing the efforts to address the so-called *global commons* or those aspects of the environment that are shared between all parts of the world or at least among large numbers of nations.[3] Efforts to control the emissions of carbon dioxide and other gases associated with climate change are a prime reflection of this, together with international efforts to control a previously unrestricted activity (releasing greenhouse gases into the environment). Second, it has encouraged environmental issues to be addressed in a more integrated fashion than they once were. This is partly captured by the idea of transferring control efforts from the *end-of-the-pipeline* to their ultimate source in the way goods and services are designed, distributed, and disposed of. It is reflected in such concepts as life cycle analysis, enterprise thinking, and *ecoeffectiveness*.[4] Third, being associated with what some have called "third wave environmentalism,"[5] sustainability has changed the extent to which the environment is presented as a limiting factor on business. In the 1970s, the environment was presented as placing a "limit to growth" that required business and people to modify their behavior in fundamental ways or risk massive upheaval as the limits of resource availability were reached. With sustainability, the message is that *green growth* is possible by shifting away from a dependence on resource-intensive technologies and limiting the use of nonrenewable resources in favor of clean technology, renewable sources of energy, smart networks, and related innovations. The broad claim is that with green growth it should be possible to decouple growth in income per capita from environmental performance.[6]

The issues of sustainability and public policy have become closely intertwined. The extent to which businesses have accepted a need to address their environmental performance is connected to the perceived cost and difficulty in doing it. A traditional view of how business has thought about their environmental responsibilities is that they are "a nuisance, or at least an impediment to profit ... a set of conditions that impede, rather than facilitate, the accumulation of wealth."[7] The contemporary view emphasizes how environmental performance can be a business opportunity that offers a "win–win" outcome rather than a constraint on profit.

Various mechanisms have been suggested that link good environmental performance to rewards in the market place, including the following[8]:

- Cost reduction: investment that reduces environmental impacts by cutting resource consumption and emissions per unit of output simultaneously raises production efficiency. This is sometimes referred to as *ecoefficiency*, the process of reducing the amount of environmental resources used to produce a product and service.[9]
- Increased revenue: addressing environmental performance can stimulate innovation and improvements in products and services that increase market share or create new demand.
- Better risk profile: a proactive stance toward environmental performance can reduce the exposure to incidents that may lead to legal prosecutions and a loss of reputation. They can help ensure the business is ahead of community expectations and so ensure a business is well positioned to adjust to any changes in the standards set by regulatory agencies.
- Enhanced reputation: beyond positive customer reaction, businesses can gain from being viewed as better places to work and better businesses to invest in than those which do not show commitment to minimizing their environmental footprint. For businesses acting as subcontractors and suppliers to businesses reliant on the performance of their supply chain, demonstrating environmental responsibility can be a prerequisite for doing business.

On the basis of these types of benefits, it has been argued that there is a business case for being a responsible business that includes sustainability in its "bottom line." If this were true it would suggest that there ought to be little need for new environmental policy, or at least that environmental policy need not be onerous or rigid in its implementation as the existence of a *business case* implies market processes will promote a transition toward more sustainable forms of economic activity. A limitation is that sustainability can only be judged for an economy as a whole or perhaps even for the planet as a whole.[10] Resource efficiency projects can make good business sense for an individual enterprise and reduce environmental impacts per unit of output, but the sustainability of the economy as a whole is not necessarily advanced by these actions. Measures taken by an individual enterprise are potentially negated by what other enterprises do and by the overall level of demand in the economy. Nonetheless, as progress toward sustainability relies on sustainable business practices being adopted, it is still relevant to examine evidence claiming to show the business case for sustainability. In practice, there is much uncertainty around how far and how smoothly business is becoming more sustainable than it was.

Questioning Business Case Sustainability

Case studies of high profile companies such as Dow Chemicals, Unilever, and Wal-Mart and of individual industries appear to show how environmental and business performances can be linked.[11] Companies increasing their reliance on environmentally certified raw materials, working with suppliers to reduce packaging or extending their production of "environmentally friendly" consumer items such as energy-efficient light bulbs are at the same time shown to be reaping considerable financial and competitive advantage. Companies are doubtless making the changes reported and individual projects may offer business advantages, but this type of evidence has four key limitations.

First, it tends to consider microprojects going on within a larger business and may not evaluate whether the business as a whole is becoming any more sustainable. Peter Dauvergne and Jane Lister have documented the efforts being made by some of the world's largest consumer goods businesses and identified that this can be viewed as a positive move toward sustainability when the immediate actions alone are considered.[12] For example, they show how companies such as Coca Cola, Ikea, McDonald's, and Walmart are helping their suppliers reduce waste, save packaging, increase their use of recycled materials, and generally lessen their environmental impacts. Nonetheless, they doubt this brings a net benefit for the environment as the motive of companies is ultimately about securing their own business growth and market dominance. What Dauvergne and Lister call "ecobusiness" are simultaneously getting their suppliers to meet sometimes ambitious sustainability targets while they themselves are aggressively marketing products such as disposable nappies, soft drinks, bottled water, and toiletries to new consumers around the world. The overall net impact is less sustainability as consumers are encouraged to purchase goods that variously displace more sustainable alternatives, facilitate unnecessary consumption, increase the overall use of resources, shift the incidence of environmental demands (for example, less cost for some goods means more income to purchase other goods) or some combination of these impacts. Similarly, whitewear manufacturers appear to demonstrate the business case for sustainability with their shift away from using ozone-depleting refrigerants (carboflurocarbons or CFCs) and their development of energy-saving refrigerators until note is taken of how these savings helped whitewear companies encourage consumers to buy more refrigerators and freezers with more storage capacity than was possible earlier.[13] Environmental gains identified in the per unit of food stored are nullified by the continuing growth in the total volume of refrigerator and freezer space in use.

Second, using the terms introduced above, the distinction between ecoefficiency (or, simply defined, "use less") and ecoeffectiveness ("do more good") needs to be considered.[14] Much of the effort going on at best involves ecoefficiency: this aims to improve the proportion between environmental resource usage and output for existing products and processes. The limitation is that efficiency impacts are subject to *rebound* effects that nullify any environmental gains. Reductions in car emissions, for example, can be neutralized by increases in vehicle ownership and car usage. This feedback mechanism has been labeled the "dilemma of the N curve."[15] Ecoefficiency centers around approaches such as reduce, reuse, and recycle that may enhance the ability to do more with less, but this alone does not stop continued erosion of the capacity of the environment to sustain economic growth. Recycling, for example, is typically *downcycling* in that it consumes energy and captures a resource that is of inferior quality to the original source material.

Ecoeffectiveness is about shifting to technologies that decouple the level of environmental impact from the level of consumption, enabling improvements in the quality of life to be sustained without damaging if not positively improving the state of the natural environment. As expressed by one advocate of ecoefficiency, the issue is not about doing the same with less but rather about doing far more with far less.[16] The challenge is that ecoeffective solutions require innovation beyond the scope of ordinary businesses including the ability to develop a market for sustainable offerings, the ability to scale a green supply network, and possibly the need to create supporting infrastructure to service the new product or service. Electric or hydrogen-powered vehicles, for example, potentially offer an ecoeffective solution to personal travel but commercial production of renewably powered vehicles will require coordinated efforts of multiple parties.

Third, the evidence drawn upon to support the existence of a business case for sustainability is chaotic.[17] Case studies report a variety of measures of business performance and relate to different types of environmental initiative, whereas they are treated as if they are measuring the same issue. Companies act in response to specific challenges and have a particular business case that they are looking to fulfill whereas aggregating case study evidence requires that the motive for acting and outcomes looked for are uniform. For example, a supermarket company may seek to enhance its environmental performance to help deflect criticism arising from the monopolistic character of their industry and to help counter threats of regulation to introduce greater competitiveness. A power company may shift to renewable energy in response to subsidies. An airline company may invest in biofuel technology and more efficient aircraft to help offset the growing cost of aviation fuel. Each is responding to different influences, prioritizing different actions and ultimately looking for different outcomes to justify the action that they take. Without being standardized, little insight is gained about which dimensions of environmental action are related to which aspects of business performance or what influences the strength and direction of this relationship. Compilations of case study evidence get around this partly by simply considering the output of the action taken (for example, the proportion of environmentally certified suppliers utilized) rather than the outcome actually being looked for (for example, maintenance of market dominance).

Quantitative studies attempting to show a link between commitment to sustainability and business performance suffer from similar limitations. There is no standard way of judging how much effort an organization has made to become more sustainable or how successful its efforts have been. There is a good deal of overlap between market growth and investment in what may be viewed as green technology: new investment is needed to support growth and by its nature new investment tends to be more efficient than old technology. This enables it to appear there is a business case for sustainability, but really it is just showing how a growth in demand facilitates investment in new technology. The best available quantitative evidence points to considerable within industry variation in the ability of plants to combine environmental improvement with increasing business success.[18] An implication is that the business case is easier to establish for a whole industry than it is for individual enterprises within the industry. For example, the airline industry has opportunity to become "greener" by modernizing the fleet used to include the latest types of fuel economy planes but not all existing airlines are equally well placed to modernize their aircraft. Similarly, at one stage, it was estimated that the top ten oil companies in the United States had environmental expenditures that varied from slightly over five to slightly over one percent of annual sales reflecting their different situations in meeting similar environmental standards.[19] An industry may be reconfigured to combine improved environmental and business performance, but there will be winners and losers in the process of adjustment both in terms of companies and localities.

Four, business cases assume there is agreement over which development direction will bring the best environmental outcomes. In practice, there are typically alternative trajectories to be followed and no certainty as to which is more guaranteed of creating a sustainable economy than another. This is illustrated, for example, in the case of the debate between fair-trade and local food consumption.[20] In high-income economies, there is support for shifting toward increased local production of food for local consumption. Citizens in low-income countries tend to see it differently with their vision of a more sustainable future frequently including greater integration into the global economy, provided this is on terms in which world trade gives room for "fair-trade." According to the Fairtrade Foundation, fair-trade schemes provide "a unique alliance for change between millions of producers in poor countries and consumers in rich countries. It has provided a living model of trade that works through the conventional market—and yet challenges its unfair rules."[21]

Industrial ecology is another illustration of the divergent agendas surrounding how to improve environmental outcomes. Industrial ecology encompasses a large set of ideas linked to the view that minimizing waste is good for the environment.[22] Moving away from linear to closed-loop industrial systems is central to the agenda with the objective of turning the effluents and wastes from one process into the input materials for other processes if they cannot be eliminated entirely.[23] Waste and pollution are indicators of uneconomic and harmful practices that should be minimized by dovetailing them with the supply of raw materials with the aim of achieving complete or near complete internal recycling of materials and "zero waste." This agenda may be contrasted with those who argue that "pollution prevention" is the more appropriate target than a focus on linking up industrial systems to facilitate the conversion and reuse of wastes.[24] Pollution prevention focuses on stopping the incidence of waste at source or at least the generation of waste that cannot be safely released into the environment. This focus, it is argued, minimizes risk partly as an unintended outcome of industrial ecology is to facilitate the continued use of harmful processes and materials as long as there is scope to recycle the waste. As well, it has been pointed out that the viability of materials interchange on any large scale has yet to be demonstrated but it is likely that the costs of closing loops will frequently exceed the benefits for the enterprises involved.[25]

Shared Value

These four issues question experience to date, but the argument nonetheless continues that it makes business sense for private enterprise to take a lead in driving change toward a more sustainable future and that this impulse should be capitalized upon before resorting to regulation. In particular, Michael Porter, an academic specializing in strategic management, and Mark Kramer, a NGO specialist, have teamed up to explore how strategy links to social responsibility.[26] They developed the concept of *shared value* to support their case that there is immense potential for the cocreation of business value complementing value for society and the environment. Their concept of shared value is presented as a challenge to the notion that addressing wider public interests is incompatible with being a profit seeking business pursuing the interests of its shareholders. Porter and Kramer see a number of trends giving space for the cocreation of business and social value: ethical consumption, *lifestyles of health and sustainability* (LOHAS), *lifestyles of voluntary simplicity* (LOVOS), Fairtrade, and a preference for locally sourced produce. As noted above, seeing only positive outcomes from these trends (whose importance is frequently exaggerated[27]) tends to side-step the uncertainty over what changes bring net positive outcomes for the environment. Moreover, even where individual "ethical" businesses are successful a "rebound" potential exists in the way an ethical purchase may concentrate a consumer's interest and help to justify the continued patronage of mainstream goods and services.[28]

The significance of the shared value concept can also be judged by the ground rules Porter and Kramer set for shared value creation. First, shared value will be created only if the scope for it is recognized at the outset of a project as otherwise initial decisions may compromise what can be delivered. Second, the shared value is identified by considering the *extended enterprise* rather than the individual enterprise: this means the entire sphere of affected parties who have some connection to the focal enterprise so-called (direct and indirect suppliers and partners, direct and indirect users, and those dealing with the "end-of-life" of the products linked to the enterprise activity). Third, managers must be sensitive to the relationships between stakeholders and be open to the opportunities for changing relationships in ways that maximize shared value rather than value to their own organization. The limitation of these guidelines is that they permit instances of shared value to be claimed where the community gain may be conditional on the responses of third parties and without the business itself having to deliver the shared value.

This relates to a larger problem with the evidence around business case sustainability: anticipated outcomes are mixed with real outcomes. Shared value can be identified with an assumption that future demand will exist and that supply chains will adapt to help build the market for green products and services. This can greatly simplify the nature of the change required.[29] Another form of anticipation is that proactive action will help businesses shape government actions and future regulatory regimes to maximize the scope for earning a return on their investment in environmental initiatives.[30] Business is also recommended to see value in placing themselves in a position where they avoid the risk of environmental incidents and liabilities. Improved risk management certainly has a financial value but precise valuation is hard to make and, more importantly, tends to focus on known and calculable risks only (an issue commented upon further in Chapter 2 in the context of risk-based regulation).[31]

Self-Regulation

The above comments are directed at individual company initiatives and may need to be modified to take note of *self-regulation*. Business contributions to sustainability potentially take on a more systematic form where they involve industry-determined standards, guidelines, and codes of conduct or practice such as the Forest Stewardship Council's forest management certification and chain of custody certification,[32] the Marine Stewardship Council fisheries standard and chain of custody standard[33] and the Equator Principles governing project financing in developing countries.[34] In addition, the United Nations has a number of initiatives in which business and other organizations are invited to join a code of conduct or adhere to a set of standards including the UN Global Compact and the Global Reporting Initiative.[35] The boundary between self-regulation and government regulation is blurred when the need to establish some form of self-regulation is mandated by law, but this still leaves a considerable number of "pure" acts of self-regulation where the initiatives come from industry itself, although influenced by the broader public policy context, which is a heightening concern with the state of the environment.

A general claim for self-regulation is that it has potential to engage the support of business more than externally imposed regulation, partly through its sensitivity to market circumstances and capacity to be informed by a detailed knowledge of the circumstances affecting business within the industry. The ability to utilize peer pressure to ensure compliance is a further reason to see value in self-regulation.[36] Against these possibilities, the reality is that it is extremely difficult to get support for industry-based initiatives.[37] Typically industry-wide agreement to a significant course of action relies upon a high degree of similarity among industry participants, a coherent set of forces, which industry participants recognize as a threat to their viability and a perceived risk of reputational contagion between industry participants regardless of their individual performance. Such requirements help to explain why the chemical industry's Responsible Care program is among the longest running examples of self-regulation (Box 1.1).

Box 1.1 Responsible Care: An Example of Self-Regulation

The Responsible Care program was started after the accident in 1984 at a factory in Bhopal, India, then partly owned by Union Carbide from the United States that killed approximately 10,000 people and may have injured up to 100,000 other people living near the plant at the time of the explosion. Responsible Care is a self-regulation initiative by the chemical industry to prevent such accidents being repeated. The goal of Responsible Care is to improve the reputation of the chemical industry by improving the environmental performance of individual chemical firms. It requires the CEO of member companies to sign up to a set of guiding principles and for the member company to implement codes of management practice covering aspects of community awareness and emergency response, pollution prevention, process and employee safety, and product stewardship. Instigated by the Canadian Chemical Producers' Association in 1985, the program has been taken up in over 50 countries. Nonetheless, by the mid-2000s, it was judged to be having little impact on public perceptions of the chemical industry.[38] One evaluation found that compared with the chemical industry as a whole, Responsible Care members in the United States tended to be worse environmental performers than nonmembers.[39] This was explained by a tendency to retain noncompliant companies as members which invites other under-performing firms to join without engendering motivation to improve their environmental performance relative to the industry as a whole. A challenge is the large number of chemical industry companies which makes informal peer pressure less effective than in industries with a relatively small number of participants.

Whatever the potential of self-regulation to deliver changes in business behavior more swiftly and with less resistance than externally imposed regulation, most academic evaluation points to it failing to deliver on this potential.[40] A recent overview of industry self-regulation directed toward environmental protection, for example, concludes that without oversight from stakeholders (including the government) attempts at self-regulation may merely substitute good feeling for good action: "If one message comes out of research on self-regulatory institutions it is that the risk of a 'conspiracy against the public' is always present."[41] Rather than not simply being effective, this claim is that self-regulation can be become a barrier to change in that the way the existence of schemes creates a diversion that hides how little action is occurring. Self-regulation is only likely to make a significant contribution to advancing sustainability when third parties from outside the industry to which the regulation applies are part of its design and implementation. This claim is consistent with evidence that much self-regulatory action is preemptive in nature, either seeking to avoid the imposition of government regulation or at least aimed at influencing the direction that it may take.

In the early 2000s, for example, around 60 large corporations were identified as having joined voluntary programs in the United States to cut their emission levels.[42] This action is a case where a form of self-regulation is informed by stakeholder expectations, but for most participants, the significance of the action was threefold:

- It gave business managers experience to assess and respond to potential regulatory policies and put them in a position to gain influence over the design of any policy that is implemented.
- Preemptive action was viewed as a way of controlling the options available to policy makers. The self-regulated action was viewed as setting a standard to be followed in any government regulated program or as a contribution to be counted when any government regulation commenced or both.

- The investment in proactive action was rationalized by it being required to be made at some stage given a context where the likelihood of government action occurring was considered high.

Such experience underlines that self-regulation does not stand alone. It can have a role to play but in a context where public agencies and other interested parties shape the form that self-regulation takes. A critical requirement being that self-regulation includes viable enforcement mechanisms and independent auditing to verify that firms are compliant with schemes that claim to demonstrate some form of environmental responsibility.

Economizing Nature

Whatever the present situation, the link between business and environmental performance will become more evident than it is at present as the use of environmental resources gets reflected in company valuations and market prices.[43] This is the perspective of *ecological modernists* who envisage a kind of *ecological switchover* taking place once environmental criteria are integrated within production and consumption processes. Post switchover, it is envisaged that economies will have reached a point on the *Kuznets curve* (named after the economist Simon Kuznets) beyond which environmental degradation declines as average per capita income continues to increase.[44] Changes in the composition of economies (that reduce the size of high pollution industries) will help make the transition, but this source of change is a stronger force for individual economies than the planet as a whole. High-income economies "export pollution" as they become more dependent on resources and manufacturing located in newly industrializing economies. Technological change in which the current dependence on nonrenewable resources is superseded by a reliance on sustainable technologies is similarly a long-term process. It is estimated, for example, that it took 50 years for the U.S. economy to shift from a dependence on coal to petroleum as its major energy source. Widespread conversion to renewable energy remains a distant prospect.

Accelerating the transition to a sustainable economy and providing certainty that this is the trajectory followed ultimately depends on "economizing ecology." This means ensuring that market prices incorporate the costs associated with the goods and services being consumed, including the use of currently uncharged for or incompletely charged for environmental services. Changing how prices for goods and services are fixed requires regulation as whatever the professed support for LOHAS and LOVAS, low (incomplete) prices tend to win over high prices—a process often described as a "race to the bottom." Regulation based simply on enforcing conformance to specified behaviors is potentially costly and time consuming. The so-called *smart regulation* is critical in helping to make the connection between environmental and business performance stronger than it currently is.[45]

Regulation is smart when it achieves change in cooperation with the parties who are best able to deliver the desired change rather than forcing change on unwilling parties, as much traditional regulation is envisaged as doing. Smart regulation is envisaged as intervention based on lighter touch controls than has been associated with traditional approaches to regulation.[46] The idea of "smart" regulation is to look to find optimal mixes of control methods that may be applied by trade associations, pressure groups, corporations, and even individuals, as well as or instead of government agencies. Smart business regulation opens up market opportunities rather than simply curtailing activity, combines strict standards with flexible implementation, and is sensitive to investment cycles (referring to the need for upfront investment to generate demand for novel products and services)[47] (Table 1.1). This sensitivity recognizes how the transition to sustainability requires investment in innovation before enforcing conformance to technologies and processes that bring better environmental outcomes than existing options. The development of the Toyota Prius hybrid car is given as an example of what can be achieved with innovation-orientated regulation arising out of Japan's "Top Runner" program.[48]

The Top Runner program encouraged the investment in the original hybrid innovation by setting energy-efficiency product standards that would help ensure demand for hybrid vehicles. This is achieved partly by setting product standards to match the highest energy consumption

Table 1.1 Jänicke's smart attributes of Japan's Top Runner Program[49]

Smart regulation attribute	Application in Top Runner
A policy instruments supports innovation by: • Economic incentives • Adding incentives to switch to innovative solutions • Including strategic planning and goal formulation • Recognizes a need to support diffusion and innovation	Innovation is helped to secure market share by setting energy-efficiency standards according to the current industry best performer (top runner). Energy-efficient products fit consumer preferences.
A policy style supports innovation by being: • Based on dialog and consensus • Calculable, reliable, and long-term • Decisive, proactive, and demanding • Open and flexible • Management orientated	Energy-efficient standards are set according to the best performance in negotiation with producers and importers. Efficiency standards are measured for the average performance of a manufacturer's or importer's products, not mandated for every product. 'Name and shame approach' is used before imposing sales restrictions.
A policy program and related actions support innovation where they: • Favor horizontal and vertical policy integration • Objectives are networked • Regulator and regulated are networked together • Relevant stakeholders are part of the policy network	The program is combined with related regulations (including a Green procurement Law and a Green automobile tax) and annual awards for energy-efficient products, energy labels and retailers of energy-efficient products.

efficiency on the market and adjusting these standards by considering potential technological improvements. A degree of flexibility is incorporated in the program by allowing manufacturers of regulated products to calculate their conformance to energy-efficiency standards as an average across their total sales. This means that sales of the highly efficient products allow the company to stay within the standard even when continuing to sell less-efficient products, giving a further reward for investing in energy-efficiency innovation.[50] Mandatory labeling of the energy-efficiency performance of regulated products and recognition of retailers as "outlets that excel at promoting energy-efficient products" are a further part of the program's efforts to help manufacturers build a market for innovative products. Market-based measures are also part of the approach to enforcement. Manufacturers and importers of product failing to meet an energy-efficient standard risk being identified publicly and then ordered to conform. Such enforcement action is tempered according to the potential impact on energy consumption in Japan and the social impact of requiring production cutbacks, the ultimate sanction available under the program. For example, limited sales of inefficient products are unlikely to attract enforcement action because it poses a low risk.

The Top Runner program deals with the energy efficiency of newly manufactured consumer products made in or imported into Japan. Its effectiveness is connected to Japan's energy environment which, as the program administrator's note, is characterized by an inherent fragility.[51] This delivers the program into a society that is generally supportive of energy conservation. Outside of this context and applied to the broader challenge of sustainable development, which must deal with more than product standards, the wider application of the Top Runner approach as a specific model of regulation is limited. It does nonetheless hold lessons for market-based policy instruments, which have been widely viewed as the smart approach to regulation. For example, as well as the Top Runner program, the European Union emissions trading scheme is viewed as another example of smart regulation.[52] Like the energy-efficiency initiative, an emission trading scheme is considered smart because it can deliver conformance to a strict target with flexible implementation procedures and market incentives.

This book is about such claims and how far the instruments that have been introduced to help business operate in more sustainable ways are really smart. As noted, market-based solutions (such as emissions trading, transferable quotas, and environmental offsets) are being viewed as ways of changing business behavior that is both effective and relatively attractive to business. This book draws on the accumulating experience of using these new approaches to environmental policy to help business managers make informed decisions around their participation in such programs and to help them assess the certainty in the future of this new policy environment. An underlying premise of the book is that alternative explanations exist for shifts in the design of public policy such as that which has overtaken environmental policy. A normative approach focuses on the choice that ought to be made according to policy theory and evidence of how policies have operated in practice. A political economy approach looks at how choices have been made in practice noting that they are not necessarily based on evidence of the relative effectiveness of alternative policy approaches. This book aligns most closely with the latter perspective: a collective desire to believe in the superiority of market-based instruments better explains their diffusion than evidence of their greater effectiveness in practice.[53] Thus, although it is possible to point to some successful uses of market-based instruments, this does not indicate that other less "business friendly" forms of regulation have become redundant. Against this context, the book aims to help business managers and prospective business managers determine their support for the new policy environment.

The book continues with further discussion of the attributes that make regulation smart and which minimize the burden on business of managing regulatory requirements. Subsequent chapters examine two approaches to environmental regulation that have been viewed as smart designs: emissions trading (including offsetting) and information sharing. Each chapter provides a guide to the objectives of policy makers and the main design decisions associated with the policy approach. The fit between policy objectives and policy experience following the two approaches is summarized to provide commentary on the effectiveness of the policy approach, potential areas of reform, and to appraise students of issues to consider in determining their engagement with the policy approach. The last chapter of the book provides an assessment of the overall contribution that smart regulation can play in promoting a shift toward a sustainable future and what other forms of action may be required by outlining six principles to guide the implementation of regulation.

Chapter Summary

Sustainable economies deliver increases in the standard of living for their citizens without degrading the state of the physical environment or depleting natural resources available to future generations. Individual businesses can contribute to the transition, but ultimately progress in becoming sustainable should be judged at the level of the economy as a whole. Business case sustainability suggests that business opportunities and market rewards provide incentives for sustainable business practices. Evidence to support this fails to consider the net impact of business strategies, does not distinguish ecoefficient from ecoeffective strategies and tends to overlook the uncertainty surrounding how environmental challenges are best responded to. The concept of shared value provides guidelines on how to align business and sustainability but anticipates potential benefits that may not be realizable in practice. An ecological switchover, in which the extent of environmental degradation is no longer proportionate to the level of economic activity, relies on economizing nature. Smart regulation is the most effective way of ensuring prices for goods and services fully reflect environmental costs and benefits. Market-based policies are considered smart: this claim forms the focus of the reminder of the book.

Key Concepts

Business case: a justification for action based on profit earning opportunities.

Business case sustainability: changes in business practice presented as contributions to sustainability justified by the potential for cost savings and income growth.

Downcycling: the tendency for resources captured through recycling to be of inferior quality than the original resource and for recycling to consume energy and resources that further mitigate the environmental gain from recycling resources.

Ecoefficiency: producing the same output with proportionately less environmental impact.

Ecoeffectiveness: redesigned products and services that reduce the environmental impacts of their production, use or disposal regardless of the level of demand.

Economizing nature: ensuring that prices charged for goods and services include paying for the use of environmental resources.

Ecological modernization: a perspective which sees that continued technological progress and economic growth provides the best means of resolving current environmental problems.

Ecological switchover: a stage in the development of economies beyond which continued economic growth brings a net reduction in environmental impacts.

End-of-the-pipeline: measures that address the management of pollution created by industrial processes; contrasted with efforts to stop the creation of pollution in the first instance.

Extended enterprise: the direct and indirect suppliers and partners, direct and indirect users, and those dealing with the end-of-life of the products linked to the activity of individual enterprises.

Global commons: natural assets important to human well-being that are outside national jurisdiction, for example, the oceans and the earth's atmosphere.

Green growth: a model promoted by the OECD (the Paris-based organization of wealthy industrial nations) that suggests the uptake of environmental technologies such as sustainable energy will allow economies to grow without causing further environmental harm.

Industrial ecology: a perspective combining ideas from ecology and business that advocates closed-loop production systems in which wastes from one activity become inputs to another.

Kuznets curve: a representation of how various social conditions vary with changes in national income that broadly sees more likelihood of environmental conditions first declining and then improving as incomes rise.

Lifestyles of health and sustainability (LOHAS): a marketing category based on values, attitudes, and actions of consumers that are attracted to goods and services by their health and sustainability attributes.

Lifestyles of voluntary simplicity (LOVOS): a movement of people who voluntarily reduce their consumption and simplify their lifestyle.

Policy: principles and intentions used to guide decision making.

Public policy: principles and intentions influencing the design of programs administered by government agencies.

Rebound effects: negative outcomes made possible by increases in ecoefficiency.

Regulation: policy instruments administered by government agencies to control specific activities, often criticized for their inflexibility and high administrative cost for both regulators and regulated.

Self-regulation: an organized group regulates the behavior of its members, typically involving adherence to rules, standards, or codes of practice determined by an industry body.

Shared value: a concept developed by Michael Porter and Mark Kramer that says business can pursue a virtuous cycle of good behavior and mutual self-interest.

Smart regulation: government agency policy instruments that support innovation and that avoid the inflexibility and high administrative cost associated with other forms of regulation.

Sustainability: derived from the Latin verb *sustinere* (to support) and describes relations that can be maintained for a very long time, or indefinitely. Applied to the environment, it refers to those forms of human and economic and cultural activity that can be conducted without long-term degradation of the resources that are used.

Sustainable development: a term introduced into modern discourse by the Brundtland Commission (1987) to describe a situation where the needs of the present generation are met without compromising the ability of future generations to meet their own needs.

Endnotes

1. Roberts (2011), p. 1.
2. This draws on the Brundtland Commission's definition of sustainability WCED (1987).
3. For a discussion of the global commons, see Blowfield and Murray (2008).
4. See Rainey (2006).
5. This term is applied to identify transitions that vary according to the perceived scope of what has previously occurred; here, the term is drawn from its application by Gouldson and Murphy (1998). A more contemporary use of the term can be found in Hoffman and Bansal (2012).

6. See discussion of the Kuznets Curve in Laasch and Conway (2015), pp. 66–8 and OECD (2011) for discussion of green growth.
7. This claim is made by Cohen (2014), p. 3, who at the same time acknowledges the corporate understanding of the environmental issue is changing.
8. Esty and Winston (2009), Epstein (2008).
9. WBCSD (1999).
10. Daly (1990).
11. See Porter and Van der Linde (1995) and Steger (2004).
12. Dauvergne and Lister (2013).
13. Dauvergne (2008), p. 119.
14. McDonough and Braungart (2002).
15. Jänicke (2008).
16. Cohen-Rosenthal (2003), p. 22.
17. Blowfield and Murray (2008), p. 134, provide a review of the limitations, in part, drawing on Salzmann et al. (2005), Steger (2004), and Székely and Knirsch (2005).
18. Salzmann et al. (2005).
19. Walley and Whitehead (1994).
20. Morgan (2010), Perry and Battisti (2011).
21. Fairtrade Foundation (2008), p. 11.
22. See Korhonen (2002) for a discussion of the origins of industrial ecology.
23. Gibbs and Deutz (2005); Barrow (2006).
24. Oldenburg and Geiser (1997); Ashford 1997.
25. Esty and Porter (1998).
26. Porter and Kramer (2006; 2011).
27. See Moscardo (2013).
28. See Perry (2014).
29. For a case study of this in the context of the Dutch potato industry see Smit et al. (2008)
30. For example, see Labatt and Maclaren (1998), Hoffman (2005), and Kruger (2005).
31. Wynn (1993) distinguishes four situations: risk, uncertainty, ignorance, and indeterminancy. Individual companies can potentially manage risk but other threats to the environment and public health

regain collective action. Perrow (1984) makes similar points through his concept of "normal accidents."

32. See ic.fsc.org/certification.4.htm
33. See www.msc.org/about-us/standards
34. See www.equator-principles.com/
35. See www.unglobalcompact.org and www.globalreporting.org; Blowfield and Murray (2012) provide a review of UN initiatives.
36. Gunningham *et al.* (1999), p. 52.
37. Barnett (2006); Battisti and Perry (2014).
38. Environmental Data Services (2005).
39. Lenox and Nash (2003).
40. For this assessment, see Braithwaite (1993), p. 91; Gunningham *et al.* (1999), p. 52; Jenkins (2001); O'Rourke (2003); Dauvergne (2008), Chapter 23.
41. King *et al.* (2012), p. 118.
42. Hoffman (2005) and Kruger (2005).
43. This argument is made by Huber (1985), Jänicke (1985), Gouldson and Murphy (1996), and Morad 2007.
44. See Laasch and Conway (2015), pp. 67–68, for a discussion of the Kuznets curve.
45. Jänicke et al. (2000); Jänicke (2008).
46. Gunningham *et al.* (1999).
47. Jänicke (2008), p. 560.
48. The Top Runner program was endorsed by the 2012 UN Conference on Sustainable Development as a model initiative for promoting green development. For this verdict and links to further information, see http://www.uncsd2012.org/index.php?page=view&type=9 9&nr=38&menu=137
49. Table is drawn from material in Jänicke (2008).
50. See Agency for Natural Resources and Energy, Ministry of Economy, Trade and Industry (2010), p. 6.
51. Agency for Natural Resources and Energy, Ministry of Economy, Trade and Industry (2010), p. 3.
52. Jänicke (2008), p. 560.
53. This verdict draws on Stavins (2003) and Sterner (2003).

CHAPTER 2

Good Regulation

Chapter 1 argued that decoupling the level of economic activity from the level of environment impacts, an indicator of the transition to a sustainable economy, will require more than voluntary action and industry-based self-regulation. Smart regulation has been advocated as a way of helping to accelerate the uptake of sustainable business practices. The idea that regulation can be smart contrasts with the tendency to view regulation as something that inevitably imposes costs on individuals and firms, that to varying degrees impedes business start-up, investment, innovation, employment, and the incentive to grow a business.[1] In the light of such concern, this chapter examines the main ways of designing regulation other than through *command and control*.

The label command and control denotes an approach based on enforcing conformance to a required performance standard and is generally thought of as the way regulation has been designed most frequently in the past. The chapter explains how this approach works and considers whether traditional regulation is characterized fairly as an approach based simply on command and control, implying a demand for uniformity, which is avoided with other ways of designing regulation. A summary of regulatory options reveals their comparative strengths and weaknesses and areas of overlap between the different ways of designing regulation rather than sharp distinctions. Chapters 3 and 4 take a closer look at the individual forms of market-based regulation, the alternative to command and control most drawn upon in response to the expanding range of environmental concerns. To commence, the chapter continues with further explanation of the need for regulation of any form.

Regulation and Market Failure

Regulation has been defined as: "the promulgation of rules by government accompanied by mechanisms for monitoring and enforcement, usually assumed to be performed through a specialist public agency."[2] This is a more restricted definition than one encompassing any government actions influencing the behavior of individuals and firms. It leaves some uncertainty as to where regulation ends and broader initiatives commence but signals a focus on regulation that is enshrined within government agency programs that ultimately impose sanctions for noncompliance. This excludes self-regulation and voluntary approaches to securing change unless such actions are part of a public agency program or linked to an explicit intention to introduce mandatory regulation.[3] Regulation, even with the restricted definition adopted, is complex in that it affects business directly and indirectly. Directly, regulation mandates prohibits or rewards the behavior of the entities within its scope; indirectly, the environment in which a business operates is changed by regulation through the way it affects the behavior of customers, suppliers, employees, infrastructure providers, and government bodies. For example, a business may be affected directly by the imposition of a charge or taxation on previously unregulated activity and indirectly in the way this changes customer and supplier perceptions of the business.

Aligning business behavior with public interest is the broad justification for regulation. This rationale raises the question as to how the public interest is identified and how it is determined whether intervention achieves its objective of aligning market processes to the public interest. These questions are answered most frequently by reference to economic theory, and more particularly *welfare economics*.

Welfare economics is based on the notion that individuals, through market mechanisms, should be relied upon to make most social decisions. The methods of analysis used by welfare economists recognize instances where markets cannot be relied upon to distribute resources efficiently. To use economists' language, there are times when markets cannot aggregate individual utility-maximizing behavior (meaning decisions to purchase or nor purchase some good or service) so as to optimize overall social welfare. When this occurs, markets are said to fail and there is a justification for government actions to supplement or replace markets.

Welfare economists recognize many sources of *market failure*, but there are a number of archetypal situations that are used to justify a need for regulation.

- Natural monopoly: in industries with large capital requirements and large economies of scale, such as railway networks and power generation, it can be difficult for new businesses to compete with established ones. Where one or a few firms dominate an industry, the lack of competition can reduce the ability of individuals to make welfare maximizing decisions.
- Imperfect information: to maximize welfare, individual decisions must be made on the basis of adequate information, but there are instances where either producers have no incentive to reveal information about their product or service or consumers do not have the expertise to evaluate the information given and instances where both failures arise.
- Externalities: these arise in relation to those costs of production that are not paid for by the producer and in relation to those benefits that are not paid for by buyers of the producer's output. Externalities are an incentive to over produce some things, where costs are avoided, and under produce things where benefits are not fully remunerated.
- Common property goods: resources that are open for anyone to draw upon risk being used unsustainably where individual decision makers maximize their current use of the resource without regard to its long-term future. This context is known as the tragedy of the commons.
- Destructive competition: competition between enterprises that causes negative side effects for employees and society may be seen as a market failure where inadequate wages and workplace investment produce living and working conditions with high social costs.

Table 2.1 Market failures and the need for environmental regulation

Market failure	Environmental application
Natural monopoly	Energy distribution networks and energy generation businesses limit opportunity for small-scale, sustainable energy technology.
Imperfect information	Producers and consumers of goods and services are directed to make "best environmental" choices on the basis of incomplete and selective information.
Externality	The production and distribution of goods with a limited useful life, either designed deliberately for a short life or through business strategies of "planned obsolescence," imposing waste management costs for the places where these goods are disposed of.
Common property resource	Use of the atmosphere and oceans as dumping grounds for waste.
Destructive competition	Barriers to the introduction of technologies with low environmental impacts when companies compete on the basis of minimizing costs.

These forms of market failure are evident in the issues addressed by existing forms of environmental regulation as well as adding to the case for regulation as part of the stimulus for change (Table 2.1). Nonetheless, while welfare economics can make a case for intervention public policy relies on more than an economic rationality. It is frequently difficult if not impossible to convert real world situations into the data needed by welfare economists to run their forms of analysis and even where they can it should not be imagined that policy makers are "won over" simply by evidence of a market failure. Policy choices are political rather than technical bound by political institutions and made by political actors, often in response to political pressures. There is much internal debate among welfare economists about the recognition of market failures and what, if anything should be the response. A brief summary of four environmental issues illustrates the complexity that regulation is required to address: vehicle emissions, waste, sustainable energy systems, and fishing.

Vehicle Emissions

Vehicles have global, regional, and local environmental impacts. The main global concern is the emission of carbon dioxide through its connection with climate change. The contribution of vehicles depends principally on the fossil carbon content of the fuel consumed, but the management of climate change is complex. It requires coordination between countries, the inclusion of multiple climate gases, and acknowledgment of the role of carbon sinks. At the regional scale, vehicle emissions can contribute to acid rain depending on the location of emissions, the mixing with other pollutants and vehicle characteristics. Locally, congestion, noise and air pollution are problems according to climate and weather conditions, vehicle characteristics, driving conditions, and fuel characteristics.

Local impacts are especially complex: exhaust emissions can pose serious health risks, but exact location matters. Inner city populations are more exposed to health risks than those outside of cities. Vehicle age also matters. The most damaging pollutants (volatile organic compounds, nitrogen oxides, and particulate matter) have reduced in the order of 5–10 times over the last decade. Future emissions are potentially much lower than present ones depending on the extent to which the vehicle fleet is renewed and how renewal changes the profile of the fleet. Engine temperature, weather, fuel, driving style, and congestion further influence the total environmental damage. In cold weather, a significant share of emissions occurs at the journey outset even if the trip is a long one. Congestion affects the rate of emissions per distance traveled and the density of emissions.

Physical (traffic management and speed controls) and regulatory measures (mandatory equipment, fuel quality, engine performance, and vehicle inspection) are the main ways of controlling the impacts of road transportation. Emission standards can be criticized for producing excessively clean cars in rural areas and insufficiently clean ones in city centers. In theory, a combination of road pricing (with pricing varied according to the location of highway, the type of vehicle and time of day) and vehicle taxes differentiated according to vehicle characteristics could give better control than imposing vehicle performance standards. Road charges linked to sophisticated monitoring technology could make it expensive to drive where and when environmental impacts are high but still not protect citizens from drivers who prefer to pay and pollute.

Waste

Products are discarded as waste because of the planned failure of materials (disposable products and short-life cheap manufactured goods), functional obsolescence (products outdated by technology), and style obsolescence (products outdated through demands generated by perceptions of good design as influenced by the creative arts, media, and the advertising industry). In the United States, these processes plus waste arising as an output of industrial processes and consumption contributed to a nearly 60 percent increase in waste generation per capita from 1960 and 1990.[4] Per capita waste generation has since stabilized with recovery rates for recycling growing to a volume equivalent to about a quarter of the waste generated. This is similar to an estimate from the World Waste Survey that across the globe around 4 billion tonnes of waste are produced annually of which around 20 percent is recovered or recycled. Discarded electrical and electronic equipment or e-waste is now a particular concern. The growing use of electronic devices for entertainment, communication, and work aligned with the high rate of equipment obsolescence has generated a huge volume of potentially toxic waste. By 2010, for example, it was estimated that 37 million computers, 17 million televisions, and 56 million mobile phones had been buried in landfills around Australia.[5]

Take-back and subsequent treatment of discarded e-waste has become the recommended strategy for dealing with the problem. The European Union Waste Electrical and Electronic Equipment (WEEE) Directive is a role model for this. This gives consumers the ability to return unwanted electrical devices back to the retailer who supplied it, with the retailer obligated to set recycling targets. This aims to optimize material recycling and to control the risks of toxic substances polluting the environment. The success of this type of approach depends on achieving high collection rates, appropriate treatment, adequate upgrading of secondary material streams, and innovation in product design to assist material reuse.

Ocean Fisheries

Oceans account for 71 percent of the earth's surface and are home to 50 percent of the world's biodiversity. Around 1 billion people depend on fish for their primary source of protein. The resource importance of the oceans has been reflected in the number and scope of international agreements to address the use and ownership of marine resources, including the UN Conventions on the Law of the Sea (UNCLOS). This law making has involved the progressive "enclosure" of the marine environment guided by the philosophy that designating clear property rights, in terms of who owns which parts of the ocean, provides a context in which environmental stewardship is more likely to be practiced than where the oceans remains an open access resource. Ongoing evidence of overfishing points to the limitations of viewing property rights as a sufficient response to a complex environmental issue.

A system of property rights that allocate entitlements to catch a certain volume of fish each season are more likely to bring positive outcomes if the catch is shared among numerous small-scale fishers than where the catch is controlled by a few big entities. With around half the world's fish stocks considered overexploited, depleted, or recovering and a further third considered over exploited, fishing effort has dispersed away from areas of the ocean within national territorial control. The further difficulty is that global environmental changes affecting the temperature of the sea, loss of sea ice, and ocean acidification are affecting fish populations in ways that are not well understood or adequately reflected in fishery management plans. Pollution is a further challenge whether originating from coastal development that imperils critical habitats for fish populations or in the way that the oceans act as the ultimate collection point for much of the world's discarded plastic. Aquaculture may help to maintain food supply from the ocean although if not well governed it can have severe impacts on the surrounding environment. Moreover, favored aquaculture species such as salmon and shrimp require large quantities of fishmeal and fish oil sourced from the capture of wild fish species that are becoming less abundant due to changes in the ocean environment.

Sustainable Energy

With more than half of global greenhouse gas emissions attributed to carbon dioxide emissions from the burning of fossil fuels, there is concern to convert energy systems to low carbon sustainable technologies. This involves more than simply changing energy generation changes. The task is complicated by the implications for distribution networks, energy users, energy-using equipment, and metering of energy use. Sustainable energy may also imply greater integration of the generation, distribution, and consumption of energy so as to secure more heat transfer to minimize the need for intermediary energy storage and transfer. Adding to the complexity of the task, governments around the world have tended to liberalize their energy markets giving control to private companies committed to existing technologies.[6]

Market-based policy measures such as emissions trading have been favored as ways to encourage a shift to alternative, noncarbon sources of energy. Previous uses of this policy approach have tended to encompass comparatively small groups of entities to achieve a comparatively modest change in production technology where a known alternative exists. The large-scale use of emissions trading across multiple economic sectors, as in the case of the European Union Emissions Trading Scheme, has led to little change in investment behavior. A prolonged Europe-wide economic slowdown has undermined carbon prices and destroyed confidence in carbon markets. Having at one stage promised a relatively painless transition in energy generation technologies, it seems unlikely that emissions trading can now play more than a secondary role (see Chapter 4). Old style, command, and control regulation has the power to promote specific technologies and enforce limits on carbon emissions, but this approach would have been easier to pursue if energy generation and distribution remained the responsibility of state-owned companies.

Economic regulators tend to have a big influence over energy markets because energy generation and distribution has a tendency to monopolistic control. Energy market regulators tend to focus on limiting profit and driving down energy prices for consumers. This can produce a degree of choice, but an environment of price controls and high competition may be discouraging of new or innovative technologies that cannot match the price competitiveness of established incumbents. In theory, it is feasible for regulators to include sustainability considerations into their calculus but the freedom to do so tends to vary according to regulatory jurisdictions. The current response to sustainability concerns includes a diversity of renewable technologies, from systems small enough to be plugged directly into individual homes to large wind farms. This brings changes for transmission and distribution systems and the need to cope with technologies that operate intermittently. Immediately, this can mean high costs and the need to address the consequences for low-income consumers.

Regulation Design

The multifaceted nature of the barriers to creating a more sustainable economy suggests the benefits of drawing upon a range of regulatory tools as part of the effort to engineer a change in business behavior. New governance regulatory techniques purport to provide smarter ways of making regulation than has previously been tried.[7] Focusing on those that have gained the most attention, the following sections provide a summary of responsive regulation, principles-based regulation, risk-based regulation, metaregulation, and market-based regulation. The discussion concentrates on differentiating overall styles of regulation with less attention on the varieties within any individual style. Before looking at these new approaches, the idea of command and control is outlined as this is frequently presented as the alternative and less desirable way of implementing regulation.

Command and Control

The environment as a public policy issue dates from the 1970s when governments in many developed countries first established environmental ministries, influenced by global dialog over the state of the environment initiated by the United Nations. As environmental ministries gained power to regulate the use of environmental resources and to control significant sources of pollution, they introduced rules and standards backed by legal enforcement powers. These include health standards based on some scientific analysis of what it takes to protect people and other living organisms from harm. Standards that impact directly on individual businesses are of two main types. *Performance standards* set a target to be adhered to either in the form of the performance expected to be achieved when engaging in a specified activity, typically some form of industrial process that generates pollution, or in the form of environmental conditions that must be attained such as minimum air quality standards.

Performance standards can envisage the use of specific pollution reduction technologies (such as the installation of air scrubbers on chimney stacks) but do not necessarily insist that the technology is installed, only that the performance level it makes possible is achieved. *Process standards* specify how a particular activity is to be conducted and are used when the monitoring of pollution levels is not feasible. For example, process standards can be specified to require certain work processes to be followed when removing hazardous substances from demolition sites.

The broad approach of setting standards backed by powers to enforce conformance was originally known as "direct regulation" but is now more often referred to as a command and control approach. This change of title emphasizes three attributes of this type of regulation:

- Standards can identify a specific target or technology that must be adhered to and this can imply that a uniform response is required from all entities covered by the regulation.
- Licenses or permits are issued to regulated activities to confirm that the permit holder has a right to operate while also outlining the limits or conditions within which operation must take place. The threat of refusal or withdrawal of the license is one of the main ways of encouraging compliance.
- Legislation may authorize a designated authority to monitor compliance and take necessary enforcement action in cases of noncompliance with the requirements of the permit.

During the 1990s, claims grew that command and control regulation is more costly and inflexible than other approaches.[8] Among the concerns, enforcing standards was said to give organizations too little opportunity to manage environmental impacts in ways tailored to their own situation. Compulsion to conform encourages resistance to the need for regulation and at best produces "end-of-pipe" solutions: action that manages impacts rather than providing incentives to redesign activities so that damage does not arise in the first place. High monitoring and enforcement costs were claimed to make industry less willing to comply than when they are able to determine how to respond to the issue of concern.

These arguments were addressed particularly to the case of environmental regulation where the command and control approach was also linked to the broadening concerns of environmental policy.[9] Enforcing standards may be sufficient when the target is to mitigate the impacts of economic activity but less so when the focus shifts to promoting sustainable forms of development. As the environmental agenda expanded, three gaps in command and control regulation were identified.[10]

- Standards and the associated regulatory agencies tend to develop incrementally. Environmental media (air, water, and land) are addressed separately as they become of concern. A fragmented control regime encourages pollution to be diverted to the weakest area of control rather than ensuring an absolute reduction of impacts.
- The incremental issue-based development of policy means that opportunities to integrate separate regulatory systems and agencies are slow to be taken, reducing the efficiency of intervention by creating policy overlaps and multiple enforcement resources.
- Policy fragmentation lends justification to the claim that legislation is confusing, sometimes establishing conflicting expectations, and hence that compliance cannot reasonably be expected.

These arguments proved influential and encouraged demand for new approaches to environmental regulation, but it is important not to overlook that command and control has strengths as well as weaknesses.

- The behavior expected is specified in the standards to be adhered to which in turn makes monitoring and enforcement comparatively straightforward. This makes the regulation dependable in terms of its ability to bring the change wanted.
- The regulation sends a comparatively strong signal that a particular action is refrained from or modified. It is effective in securing change when any exemptions are understood as concessions, rather than suggesting an entitlement, and the need for the regulation has public support.

- Where businesses are required to act in similar ways, it can stimulate environmental management services to assist compliance with regulation based on the large market opportunity. Business responses that involve technological and managerial improvements may ultimately assist international competiveness against businesses that have not been stimulated to act.

It should be also recognized that what became labeled as command and control actually encompassed regulation that was more variable than simply requiring conformance to a uniform standard. The so-called *new governance* techniques encompass aspects of the way regulation has always been more diverse in approach than advocates of alternative modes of regulation may admit. For example, environmental management has in the past made use of performance-based standards that allow businesses to determine how best to meet the mandated performance level without proscribing how they do so. This avoids the major criticism of command and control as requiring a standard response that does not take into account what is cheapest and most effective for the individual entity being regulated. The need to obtain planning or resource consent prior to developing land or rebuilding on an already developed site is a form of environmental regulation found in most developed economies. Urban planning systems vary in their reliance on zoning rules versus performance-based guidelines, but generally, there is some scope for determining development applications by reference to the desired quality of the environment that needs to be protected (such as a level of water and air quality to be maintained, the level of visual amenity value sought and conservation of ecosystem processes) rather than specifying how each unit of land can be used.[11]

Nonetheless experimentation with alternative approaches to regulation has occurred and has been linked to claims of growing business support for sustainability. The chapter goes on to summarize the main approaches that have been viewed as offering a smarter way of designing regulation than relying on command and control approaches. While presented as alternative forms of regulation all approaches are built around four basic components: target, regulator, *command*, and *consequence*.[12]

Applied to environmental regulation, business organizations are the primary target although regulation may vary according to its coverage of some business sectors only and according to whether it encompasses more than private enterprise. The regulator is generally a government agency with some variation in the use of third parties to assist compliance.

The nature of the command and the consequence are the main sources of difference (Table 2.2). The command identifies what the regulation requires affected parties to do or refrain from doing. Commands

Table 2.2 Comparing regulation design

Regulation design	Main variations	Command	Consequence
Command and control	Performance standard	Attain specified level of performance	Variable penalties for non compliance
	Process standard	Follow specified methods/procedures	Variable penalties for non compliance
Responsive		Varies with extent of cooperation displayed	Vary from rewards to penalties
Risk-based		Contain risk to acceptable levels	Varies with the level of risk
Principle-based	Formal	Follow specified principle	Variable penalties for non compliance
	Substantive	Show consistency with specified principle	Variable penalties for non compliance
	Networked	Show involvement with external parties in enacting specified principle	Variable penalties for non compliance
Meta		Enact preferred management systems	Variable penalties for non compliance
Market-based	Taxation	Payment for pollution generated	Financial cost/saving
	Tradable permits	Hold permits to cover the volume of pollution generated	Financial cost/saving
	Information disclosure	Release specified information to specified audiences	Potentially penalties from regulatory agency and from public pressure

can be distinguished according to whether they relate to means (actions to be taken) or ends (specification of a target to achieve) and according to whether the command is specific (attaining a precise level of performance or conforming to a specified process) or general in nature. A general means-command allows for some flexibility in the process to be adhered to; a general ends-command allows for a range of acceptable performance levels.

Consequences vary in the severity of the penalty and the certainty that they will be imposed if commands are not met. Consequences can be positive or negative. A positive consequence may be exemption from certain further aspects of the regulation or some form of financial reward. Negative consequences include fines, imprisonment, and sanctions affecting the ability to continue to conduct a business. A failure to receive a positive reward is another form of negative outcome, as where competitors obtain concessions from further aspects of the regulation that are not afforded to all parties covered by the regulation. The nature of the consequence interacts with nature of the commands to shape the overall imposition of the regulation: a specific performance command has a degree of flexibility where the consequence for noncompliance is mild.

Responsive Regulation

Responsive regulation is distinguished by its approach to the consequence of regulation. The form that the command takes is not considered except that the approach implies the use of an ultimate sanction consistent with command and control regulation. Responsive regulation follows a "tit-for-tat" model of how enterprises respond to regulatory demands and it is this element that provides the distinctive aspect of a responsive design.[13] Assuming regulator and regulated are in a long-term relationship and that regulation is something that offers long-term benefits (for example, by avoiding the need to pay for cleaning up environmental damage) in return for the immediate costs of complying, the model justifies starting with "light handed" consequences. Parties that cooperate and endeavor to comply are rewarded by the regulator's efforts to make compliance easy and by the promise of an ongoing light touch from the regulator. For the parties that do not comply, penalties escalate as they continue to desist from cooperating with regulators. Assuming the regulated entity is a rational, profit maximizing decision maker they should wish to gain the benefit of a cooperative relationship with the regulator and so be persuaded to comply even if the need for the regulation is questioned. Responsive regulation builds on this ideal reciprocal or tit-for-tat adjustment between enforcement and cooperation.

An enforcement pyramid guides responsive regulation (Figure 2.1). At the base of the pyramid, recognizing that most people and organizations wish to comply with regulation, agencies make regulation as easy as possible to comply with such as by providing easy to lodge compliance documents. Mid pyramid, where compliance is mixed despite a willingness to comply, regulators are directed to offer various forms of assistance such as guidance material and education programs. Closer to the peak of the pyramid, a prosecution process starts against those deliberately not wishing to comply, making them aware of the action that has been taken against others and then moving on to enforcement. This enforcement action seeks to secure compliance by appealing to self-interest in the form of the savings in time and effort that will result from becoming compliant. Finally, regulators may need to deal with a group who have made a positive decision not to comply and against whom they are recommended to use all forms of legal action available.

The strategic disposition of monitoring and enforcement effort is now sometimes presented in terms of the voluntary, assisted, directed, enforced (VADE) compliance model. As with the enforcement pyramid,

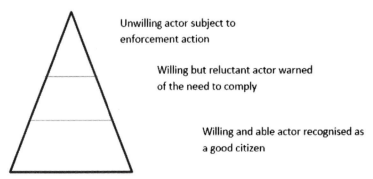

Figure 2.1 Pyramid of enforcement options with responsive regulation[14]

with VADE regulators follow a hierarchy of actions from cooperative to punitive recognizing that a strategy based entirely on persuasion will be exploited by those entities that prioritize self-interest over the long-term gains targeted by regulation. Similarly, exclusive reliance on enforcement will undermine the goodwill of entities that recognize the public good justification for regulation and entrenches the opposition of those who do not. The mixed enforcement strategy makes maximum use of persuasion, which is cheaper than pursuing compliance through punishment.

Consistent with the theory of responsive regulation, compliance has been shown to be affected by judgments of self-interest and from adherence to social norms[15] and that compliance increases where regulation is perceived as "common sense" or where guidance is perceived as readily available and easy to understand.[16] The clarity of aims and language; ease of understanding the regulation; volume of detail to be comprehended; rapidity of change; guidance on compliance; effectiveness of inspection and enforcement institutions; and nature and extent of sanctions for noncompliance influence the perception of whether the regulation should be complied with.[17] The case for responsive regulation is also supported by studies identifying archetypal attitudes to compliance, each of which suggests a different enforcement strategy: the "unaware"[18]; the "avoider"[19]; those in "vulnerable compliance" uncertain whether they are in compliance[20]; and "proactive learners" that treat regulatory interventions as opportunities for learning and improvement.[21]

Nonetheless, four limitations place practical limits on the ability to use an exclusively responsive approach to regulation.

- First, its use does not suit issues where absolute compliance is important, for example, involving the use of potentially lethal substances that need to be banned outright. Neither does it suit issues where there is need to gather information around incidents that may give rise to the need for enforcement. For example, the ability to understand industrial accidents will reduce where organizations are deterred from openly reporting incidents because the threat of enforcement exists.
- Second, business managers have an imperfect understanding of how a regulator has interacted with other regulated

parties, in some cases, because there is little interaction around which to form an impression of how the regulator responds to different levels of compliance. Among managers of small- and medium-sized enterprises (SMEs), it has been shown that there is a preference for consistently enforced regulation to ensure a "level playing field."[22] SME owners and managers tend to have little confidence that regulators behave consistently giving rise to suspicion that other SMEs get away without complying. In addition, regulator behavior is often a small influence on how organizations respond to regulation: industry culture, levels of competition, and profitability are among other influences shaping responses to regulation.[23]

- Third, in the context of industries comprised of thousands of individual enterprises, an extraordinary amount of monitoring and enforcement effort is required to generate the conditions in which the enforcement pyramid operates as depicted in theory.[24] This is especially where regulators have few tools to employ in the middle ground of incomplete compliance, leaving a choice of allowing noncompliance to continue or of taking a prosecution.[25]
- Four, there is a risk of regulators being encouraged to focus on an escalating pyramid of enforcement options rather than scanning sideways for alternative tools that may be used at the same level of enforcement.[26]

A further question is whether responsiveness is a separate style of regulation so much as a way of making use of a variety of other forms of regulation. Legal enforcement and significant penalties for noncompliance are the sanctions that arguably most motivate action at the bottom of the pyramid. Applied to command and control regulation, as noted above, a gap can exist in the middle ground of an enforcement pyramid. As discussed in Chapter 6, a pathway from weak to strong enforcement may involve shifting from one style of regulation rather than simply escalating the enforcement draw on needs to be mapped from the outset if the responsive approach is to be effective.

Risk-Based Regulation

Risk-based regulation was devised to help regulatory authorities allocate enforcement effort. It starts from the proposition that regulation is ultimately about controlling adverse impacts arising from some resource use or other behavior. To this end, regulators should evaluate regulated entities in terms of the risks they pose to achieving the objectives desired by the regulation. In the environmental context, for example, climate change is now considered a risk to human society that should be mitigated. Risk-based regulation would develop a system for assessing and scoring risks to the occurrence of climate change, evaluating sources of risk according to their gravity and likelihood of occurring. The risk assessment might also consider the intrinsic risk of the action (that which exists even under best management conditions) and operational risks that depend on the quality of control and management systems. Risk scoring provides a means of prioritizing the use of regulator resources with, for example, monitoring and enforcement effort concentrated on the entities posing the most risk. In some applications of a risk-based approach, risk scores may also be used to select the regulation strategy (education, persuasion, and sanctions).

A risk-based approach has appeared to provide an evidence-based means of targeting the use of resources and prioritizing attention to the sources of risk.[27] Setting priorities on an apparently objective risk-analysis basis, the approach appears to be transparent, systematic, and defensible. Interest in the approach was encouraged by the perception it would contribute to a significant lessening of the compliance cost of regulation. In practice, the technique is information-intensive, because targeting enforcement according to assessments of risk requires considerable intelligence as to where risk lies. This insight can be gathered through inspections and other ways of gathering data and an acceptance among regulated entities of the need to share information with regulators.[28] More problematic, risk is too complex a phenomenon to be easily operationalized in the design of regulation.

The former U.S. Secretary of Defense speaking in the context of the justification for military action in Iraq summarized how the issue of risk presents formidable analytical challenges.

Reports that say something hasn't happened are always interesting to me, because as we know, there are known knowns; these are things we know we know. We also know there are known unknowns; that is to say we know there are some things we do not know. But there are also unknown unknowns—the ones we don't know we don't know.[29]

A possibly adventurous comment for a politician, this observation fits academic commentary that recognizes how risk is one situation in a larger typology of related possibilities (Table 2.3). Risk can be calculated where the consequences of an event or decision are known and it is possible to calculate the chance of the consequences being experienced. Arguably the riskier situations are where the risk cannot be calculated.

Uncertainty exists where the consequences of an action are known but there is insufficient understanding to be able to calculate the probability of the risks occurring. Many environmental issues are of this nature: it is known that a chemical is potentially lethal but there is typically incomplete understanding of the circumstances under which its use or disposal is capable of triggering adverse outcomes. Even when the risks of something going wrong are well understood, risk analysis is still influenced by judgments over how different outcomes are valued (Box 2.1). The weight to give low-probability events with potentially catastrophic impacts is an ongoing challenge in risk analysis, known as dealing with the fat-tail problem. Calculations of the potential cost of risk events occurring are skewed by the inclusion of scenarios with catastrophic outcomes. Similarly, the

Table 2.3 Typology of risk[30]

	Consequence	Probability of consequence occurring
Certainty	Known	100 percent, if the action is taken the consequence is certain to occur
Risk	Known	Probability of the consequence can be estimated
Uncertainty	Known	Probability of the consequence cannot be estimated as too little is known about the circumstances giving rise to the consequence
Ignorance or wicked problems	Unknown	Probability of the consequence cannot be estimated because all circumstances generating risk have yet to be revealed

potential cost of extreme weather events in the Gulf of Mexico varies hugely according to whether the case of Hurricane Katrina is included or excluded on the grounds such a severe event is unlikely to be encountered again.

The "unknown unknowns" are an even greater challenge to placing regulation on a risk assessment basis, when it is not known the risks exist and so there is no way of determining their likelihood. Such situations have been called "wicked problems" for the way that environmental issues have come to light only after problems are recognized, as in the way the use of CFCs became linked to the integrity of the atmosphere's ozone layer only after damage to the layer was identified. No risk analysis had

Box 2.1 Framing Risk Analysis[31]

People's assessment of risk varies according to how risks are framed: people tend to opt for the most certain outcome when it involves a positive reward (rather than gamble on getting a higher but more uncertain reward) whereas they are more inclined to gamble on the least worst outcome occurring and disregard that it is less likely to occur than a more disadvantageous outcome. This inconsistency means that the way risks are presented can influence how they are evaluated. Beyond the difference in the way people tend to judge gains differently from losses, the selection of risk measures is rarely unbiased.

Fatality risks associated with the manufacturing of chemicals can be measured in terms of death rates (which may be calculated relative to production volumes or the population exposed to risk) and in terms of the impact on life expectancy of those affected directly or indirectly as well. Reduction in life expectancy treats deaths of young people as more important than deaths of older people who have a shorter remaining life expectancy. Simply counting fatalities treats the deaths of young and old as equivalent and does not distinguish immediate from delayed deaths. The number of deaths does not distinguish the deaths of those who were aware of the risk (and possibility gained benefit from it) from those who were exposed to the risk involuntarily without any offsetting benefit.

been conducted to inform regulation governing the use CFCs because the risks were unknown until after the hole in the atmosphere's ozone layer was identified.

At best, therefore, risk-based regulation offers an approach for addressing simple and well understood issues. Even then public perceptions are likely to skew risk-based calculations. For example, in the United States, there are close to 40,000 traffic deaths a year. These deaths are tolerated partly because of public perceptions about the risks associated with road driving: a much smaller number of deaths from air travel elicit a much higher level of anxiety and lower risk tolerance. Similarly, public concern is much higher about quick-onset risks (for example, exposure to nuclear radiation) than delayed-onset risks (for example, exposure to toxic substances that elevate the risk of cancer in later life). Risk management experts can deploy techniques to identify equivalent death rates, but this will not necessarily translate into regulation priorities accepted by those being regulated. With many risks being unknown and/or immeasurable, risk-based regulation is ultimately more an art than a science. It can fit with a public policy agenda that views risk as a personal responsibility rather than something requiring intervention in business behavior.[32] Alternatively, a focus on risk can justify highly interventionist strategies designed to minimize the susceptibility to wicked problems.[33]

Principle-Based Regulation

Principle-based regulation (PBR) fits with "new governance" forms of regulation with its central feature of providing a framework in which firms and other regulated entities can organize their own processes to achieve the outcomes the regulator seeks. Principles identify outcomes to be achieved without specifying the detailed processes for achieving them. This is intended to give room for local or "bottom up" elaboration and customization of regulation and to overcome the problems of scale that affects all regulatory regimes, namely, that the rules are promulgated to fit the economy as a whole but must be complied with in individual situations that may not fit the conditions applying in aggregate. In return for their flexibility, the regulator seeks to encourage regulated parties to see reason to go beyond minimal compliance with the requirements of regulation. To help achieve this outcome, principle-based regulation includes effort to engage regulated parties in discussions as to the broader purpose of the regulation and the types of response that it suggests will help ensure regulated entities stay ahead of the regulation. As further fits this objective, the regulator may make use of third parties such as business and trade associations to help distribute guidance on the best means of conforming to the regulation. These broad characteristics can be applied with varying degrees of effort to translate the meaning of principles for application in individual cases, creating three subforms of regulation: formal, substantive, and polycentric PBR.[34]

Formal PBR prescribes a general, broadly stated principle or more likely set of principles that indicate how regulated parties must conduct their affairs. This is a principle-based approach in that it seeks to set out the fundamental obligations that are expected to be adhered to. Some or all of the following characteristics are likely to be present:

- They are drafted at a high level of generality.
- They are qualitative rather than quantitative and mainly identify behavioral standards, such as a need to act with "integrity," "skill care and diligence," and "reasonable care" and to treat customers and manage conflicts of interest fairly.
- They are purposive and explain why the behavior is sought and not simply what behavior is required.

A trade-off exists in terms of principles that are of clear and certain meaning and those that are uncertain and allow for a margin of interpretation. The more precision of meaning and certainty of outcome are sought, the more complex they need to be to allow for all possible contingencies. Adding to the complication, precision alone does not guarantee certainty of outcome. A shared understanding between regulator and regulated is also required. This can be helped by drafting precise principles but as they become more precise so they tend to grow in complexity (as indicated by the number of subclauses, conditions, and options), which then becomes a barrier to obtaining a certain outcome. In brief, it proves very difficult to draft principles in a way that guarantees understanding of how to give effect to them.

Substantive PBR is a response to the difficulty of relying on formal principles alone to achieve the goals of regulation. Substantive PBR makes deliberate effort to develop the mutuality, trust, and reciprocity between the agency responsible for the regulation and regulated that is perceived to be the key benefit of this approach to regulation. This is pursued by a particular mode of interpretation, a particular enforcement style, an orientation to outcomes, a reallocation of responsibilities for working out the practical application of the provisions, and an explicit and developed reliance on management-based regulation (also known as metaregulation, see below). In short, with substantive PBR, there is significant effort to discuss the regulation's intent with regulated entities, including some expectation that the affected entities take a role in determining how they apply in individual circumstances. The discretion afforded firms in working out what constitutes compliance has potential to create tension between them and the regulator. Typically, firms want specific guidance whereas regulators think firms should themselves determine what action is needed. This difference of expectation can occur with any form of regulation, but with substantive PBR, there is a significant shift in responsibility to firms, which has implications for the skills of the enforcement and monitoring staff employed by regulatory agencies.

A third variety of principle-based regulation, known as polycentric or *networked PBR* combines substantive PBR with the greater use of third parties to help produce guidance on the meaning and application of the principles. This form of PBR can be viewed as a specific instance of a larger regulatory strategy of enrolling *gatekeepers* to assist promote adherence to regulation. A networked approach to responsive regulation has, for example, been discussed as a way of helping regulators engage with industries comprised of large numbers of small business. Gatekeepers in this context are parties not directly the subject of regulation but who have some position of influence over the regulated party, such as financial auditors, insurance companies, and standards agencies. It can seem helpful to draw on the role such parties play in facilitating responsible management practices. A limitation is that the third parties that are financially dependent on their clients may not be sufficiently independent to play a surveillance role for regulators. Consequently, as well as gatekeepers, there has been interest in the possible role that large, multinational companies may play in policing the enterprises that are linked to their supply chains. Further comment on this is made in Chapter 5.

The central challenge in applying a principle-based approach is that short of working perfectly as intended the opposite of what was intended is the most likely outcome. London School of Economics professor Julia Black discusses this in terms of seven paradoxes of the technique of which several are connected to the need to achieve a clear and unified interpretation of what is expected while encouraging participation and dialog over the meaning of principles. This broad area of doubt that principles are capable of bringing desired changes in behavior is illustrated by the debate around one principle that has been incorporated into environmental regulation: the precautionary principle (Box 2.2).

Box 2.2 The Precautionary Principle

Dealing with risks that have not been scientifically proven to exist but which have potentially catastrophic outcomes if they do occur is a challenge for risk-based regulation. Environmentalists tend to favor following the precautionary principle: this implies a decision rule, which says that where there are threats of serious or irreversible environmental damage, the absence of scientific proof is not a reason for postponing action to prevent risk occurring.

The precautionary principle is justified by ecological theory, which says that ecosystems tend to adjust to stress in a nonlinear fashion: pressure on ecosystem tends to result in sudden, large-scale adjustment rather than continuous incremental adaptation. It thus makes sense to act early because waiting until the environment shows sign of stress is too late to arrest the change. It can be contrasted with other decision rules for coping with uncertainty, such as acting on the balance of evidence, acting only when there is scientific suspicion of risk or when the issue is beyond reasonable doubt. The precautionary principle has been incorporated in environmental treaties and legislation and is endorsed by the European Environment Agency but has been less used in the United States.[35]

The principle alone does not identify how to deal with uncertain risks.[36] Some see the principles more as work-in-progress than as something that is ready to be applied in regulation with agreement needed on the answers to four questions.

1. To what types of hazard does the principle apply?
2. How much scientific uncertainty is required to evoke the principle (to recognize that there is rarely an absence of some degree of uncertainty)?
3. What types of measures against potential hazards does the principle refer to?
4. Are the recommended measures to be mandatory or is compliance voluntary?

For the present, the use of the principle attracts a wide range of interpretations. It can be taken to mean little more than the good sense of taking thoughtful action in advance of scientific proof. At the other extreme, it can be used to justify a shift in the burden of proof on to those who propose developments that have uncertain risks rather than the burden of proof resting on those who oppose development.

One of the paradoxes of principle-based regulation is the uncertainty whether it is helpful for principles to have an agreed, precise meaning. Where total agreement exists, a policy regime based on principles can become similar in effect to a regime characterized by detailed rules. Moreover, a desire to make principles open to interpretation, so as to enable their application to a wide variety of circumstances may be defeated by other forces encouraging uniformity. Uncertainty encourages regulated parties to seek guidance on compliance from outside consultants and advisors whose business models tend to rely on prescribing a limited range of packaged responses.[37] Consequently, whether the flexibility promised by principle-based regulation can actually encourage businesses to go beyond simply complying with regulation is unclear. Where it is not clear what specific steps need to be taken, managers may ask "can we get away with this?" rather than "is this the right thing to do?"[38]

Metaregulation

With *metaregulation*, regulators require that regulated parties develop internal management systems that are consistent with delivering the outcomes sought by the regulation. The onus is placed on regulated parties to demonstrate that their management systems and processes are fit for purpose. This gives firms opportunity to design their own processes that fit their own organization better than having to follow generic, prescriptive rules specified by the regulator. This offers flexibility, but it is associated with placing the responsibility on firms to demonstrate their compliance rather than the onus being on regulators to demonstrate noncompliance. By building the goals of regulation into internal management systems, regulators hope that their concerns are pursued without the need for continuous surveillance, and in this way, the use of metaregulation is often presented as a form of self-regulation.[39] The development of management systems certified to international standards has been viewed as a supportive development for metaregulation (Box 2.3).

Box 2.3 ISO Standards as Metaregulation

The International Standards Organization (ISO) came to prominence as a potential aid to improving the sustainability performance of companies through the release of its ISO14001 standard for environmental management systems in 1996. Offering a management system that any organization could adopt to bring its environmental impacts under control, with certification to endorse the reliability of approved environmental management systems a significant step forward was claimed. Subsequently, ISO has replicated this approach with standards for environmental audits, ecodesign principles, greenhouse gas measurement, life cycle assessments, ecoefficiency assessment, environmental labels and declarations, and social responsibility. This suite of standardized management processes offers some assurance that an issue is being addressed in a coherent and internationally consistent way. Nonetheless, ISO environmental standards have failed to demonstrate that they have potential to act as an alternative form of regulation that reduces a need for governmental action.

- The process through which standards are developed is based on countries supporting their own representatives to participate in technical committees. This tends to provide a context in which the interests of wealthier economies with well-organized industry interests dominate rather than standards pursuing sustainability in a rigorous way. This is reflected in the depiction of ISO14001 as "a missed opportunity for sustainable global industrial development."[40]
- The uptake of ISO environmental standards has not kept pace with the growth of business interest in sustainability. In 2011, China recorded slightly over 60,000 ISO14001-covered business sites compared with less than 5,000 in the United States. In Europe, Romania had 50 percent more certified sites than Germany.[41] These data reflect how ISO standards can have a role in places with weak environmental standards but offer less in economies with stronger regulatory systems.
- Uncertainty exists over the seriousness with which standards are adhered to once certification is obtained. With devolved regulation, maintaining adherence to management standards tends to rely on the presence of strong industry bodies that recognize their industry is as strong as its weakest link. ISO has generally lacked this linkage to industry groups who are motivated to ensure that certification is followed by an appropriate investment of resources.[42]

In an ideal situation, the management system sought by the metaregulation is integrated into the core processes of the business rather than it being a parallel system introduced for the purposes of demonstrating compliance. Where the systems run in parallel, there is a danger that the one introduced to satisfy a regulatory agency is subsidiary to the organization's core operations. In this context, effective metaregulation can depend on the organization having a business culture and incentive structure that respects the importance of the issues addressed in the parallel management system as well as regulators having the insight and skills to interrogate managers over the status of the parallel system.

The regulation of health and safety has been identified as a successful use of metaregulation.[43] Following the explosion and fatalities on the Deepwater Horizon oil platform in the Gulf of Mexico, the suggestion was made that based on experience in Canada, Norway, and the UK regulation allowing companies to develop their own safety plans is more effective than a prescriptive approach. The prescriptive approach governing the Deepwater Horizon platform is alleged to have created hostility between the regulators and the operators of the platform and placed the onus on the regulator to ensure health and safety practices keep up with changes in the operating environment. It remains uncertain whether metaregulation would have brought a different outcome but the incident does underline the importance of operators proactively updating their safety procedures in the light of operational changes. The regulators are not well positioned to maintain surveillance that requires up-to-date and comprehensive insight into the internal operations of individual businesses, providing a context where metaregulation can be an effective approach.

Market-Based Regulation

As the critique of command and control gained momentum in the 1980s, the original search for an alternative approach to environmental regulation settled on *market-based* instruments.[44] The context for this was the broad shift in governance philosophies in Western economies that celebrated free markets and minimum government regulation, but as the advocacy for and experimentation with market-based tools grew, so did the parties seeing benefit in this approach. In the United States, for example, the Environmental Defense Fund was one of the influential environmental lobbies to embrace market mechanisms stepping out of line with other environmental campaigners who viewed market mechanisms as variously sanctioning payment for pollution or substituting weak for strong control.[45] As market mechanisms became the preferred regulatory option in the judgments of many government regulators, business leaders, and environmental campaigners, some commentators spoke of them forming the basis for "third wave environmentalism." While in the past the environment was presented as setting "limits to growth," market-based instruments formed part of the larger argument that business and environmental interests could be brought together.

The major claim for economic or market-based instruments is that they focus mitigation efforts on organizations that are able to make the most change at least cost. If this is achieved, it means that the environment is protected at least overall cost to society. This quality of economic instruments is frequently contrasted with the way command and control approaches seek to equalize the environmental standards adhered to across all organizations. Rather than equalizing the standard attained by each individual organization, economic instruments focus on the overall environmental performance of an economy as a whole and seek to equalize the expenditure regulated organizations must make for this desired level of environmental protection to be obtained. The underlying justification is that it is not necessary to force all polluters to stop polluting as long as there are some who are able to greatly reduce their environmental impacts so that pollution as a whole goes down.

There are three main types of economic instrument, each of which gives rise to a number of subcategories (Table 2.4). Price-based instruments use some form of payment to compensate for the environmental

Table 2.4 Varieties of economic instruments[46]

Instrument type	Main features	Variants
Price-based	Influence decision making by imposing financial charges for environmental impacts and providing financial incentives for environmental improvements.	Environmental charges and taxes Incentive payments Tender for grant/subsidy payments
Quantity-based	Set a limit to the volume of emissions or other environmental impacts and then allowing the transfer of reduction effort among the regulated organizations.	Emissions trading
Market friction reduction	Increase information availability so that consumers and producers can more fully and easily identify the environmental costs of their decisions.	Labeling Public disclosure

damage caused by the activity or to discourage the activity or to achieve some combination of these outcomes. A reverse price-based instrument uses financial payments to induce a preferred action. Quantity-based instruments involve some form of emissions trading, which combine some form of quantitative target with economic incentives to bring activity within the target. This approach reduces some of the uncertainties associated with price-based instruments, but it does mean there is need for administrative rules to set the context in which economic incentives are allowed to influence mitigation effort. Encouraging information disclosure is a third type of economic instrument in the sense that market processes are enabled to work when there is fuller information available about the overall costs and benefits of supplying a good or service. Information disclosure programs aim to capitalize on this by labeling requirements and through other forms of public disclosure and reporting schemes.

With respect to the environment and smart regulation, the various forms of market-based instrument have been the main types of new governance pursued. Given this, Chapters 3 and 4 examine two forms of market instrument that have been claimed to improve on alternative approaches: emissions trading and information disclosure. Before examining these individual approaches, two broad issues indicate some of the ways that market-based environmental regulation has raised unforeseen challenges.

First, the main impact of the interest in market-based instruments has been in encouraging the use of various forms of environmental tax or charge that fall short of the full-blown implementation of a market-based tool. Taxation-based programs have typically imposed a payment, but at a level which merely signals that an activity has unwelcomed impacts and perhaps goes as far as deterring some participants from engaging in the activity at the rate they have done in the past. In a strict sense, this falls short of true market-based regulation as it does not impose a cost that equates to the level of damage caused and is not agnostic whether polluters desist from the action or chose to pay the charge and continue to pollute. One reason for the partial implementation is the concern that the strict use of market-based regulation would be at the cost of international business competitiveness. Australia and New Zealand, for example, failed to sustain carbon taxes because of political opposition based partly on concern for the impact on business of a cost not faced by overseas competitors. In the early 1990s, the European Union drew back from introducing a carbon tax because of concern that it would conflict with World Trade Organization rules, although some individual countries progressed their own taxes.

Second, programs have frequently incorporated flexible implementation and compliance rules that again have reduced the effectiveness of the programs. This has been a feature of emissions trading programs that include bubble and offsetting provisions. Treating facilities as if they were encased in a bubble means that the net emissions of the facility are considered not the emissions from each and every separate emission point within the facility. Offsetting goes further by allowing the purchase of pollution credits from outside the controlled activity to be accepted as at least a partial way of satisfying the requirements of the program. These concessions have made programs more palatable to those parties directly affected by them but they have introduced a need for close monitoring of the concession mechanisms. This undermines the intention to introduce regulation that is largely self-managing and exposed the programs to risks arising from the incentives to create offset projects. As discussed further in Chapter 4, this has particularly weakened the use of emission trading to control carbon emissions. In the absence of the strong administrative oversight needed to make sure that only environmentally sound projects are accepted within the reach of trading schemes, a "race-to-the-bottom" has been experienced.[47]

Chapter Summary

The complex nature of environmental issues suggests the importance of drawing from a range of regulatory tools rather than following a standard and uniform approach. This possibility has tended to be discussed in terms of the comparative inflexibility and resource-intensive nature of command and control versus responses that give more opportunity for business to respond to regulatory concerns in ways that best suit their particular situation. All forms of regulation include some form of command and consequence. Alternative forms of regulation are variants of the command and control approach rather than being fundamentally different. Market-based instruments offer the greatest contrast and have been the major source of policy innovation although in practice they too have typically relied upon administrative rules that lessen their distinctiveness. In this context, as the final chapter explains, smart regulation is about deploying policy instruments in ways that combine the emphasis of different approaches rather than selecting a single best form of regulation.

Key Concepts

Command: the requirement imposed by regulation.

Command and control: a form of regulation that is based on requiring all entities covered by the regulation to adhere to a set standard or face enforcement action for not doing so. Generally viewed as an inflexible and costly way of designing regulation, but this can overlook the variety of ways standards can be set and the responsive ways in which compliance with regulation can be pursued.

Consequence: the action taken by regulatory agencies when regulation is not complied with.

Formal PBR: an approach to principle-based regulation that is limited to setting out the principles regulated parties are expected to comply with.

Gatekeepers: organizations or persons that control access to resources required by businesses.

Market-based regulation: the use of economic incentives to change business behavior comprising price, quantity, and information-based forms of regulation.

Market failure: a situation where free market processes do not result in the best outcomes for society as a whole.

Metaregulation: an approach to regulation, which specifies management structures and systems to put in place to deliver performance outcomes sought by regulatory agencies.

Networked PBR: an approach to principle-based regulation that draws upon third parties to help communicate how organizations should behave to demonstrate their compliance with the principles regulated parties are expected to comply with.

New governance: a term applied to the ways of designing regulation proposed in recent decades to make regulation more efficient and effective than command and control approaches.

Performance standard: the properties required of a product or production process.

Principle-based regulation: an approach to regulation that outlines principles of expected conduct; expected to be expressed in terms that give flexibility in determining the required action.

Process standard: specification of the standards expected to be followed when conducting a management task or production process.

Responsive regulation: an approach to enforcing action is which regulatory agencies match their enforcement action with the willingness and ability of regulated parties to comply.

Risk-based regulation: an approach to regulation that targets entities posing the greatest risk.

Substantive PBR: an approach to principle-based regulation that relies upon the assistance of third parties to interpret and communicate the implications of principles of expected conduct.

Welfare economics: a theory of economics that is rooted in the belief that individual economic actors based largely on self-interest usually make decisions that are in society's best interests.

Endnotes

1. See Boyfield (2009).
2. Black (2002).
3. A motivation for self-regulation is to forestall the introduction of regulation by a public agency or to influence its design before it is being introduced.
4. Ali (2009).
5. Lehmann and Crocker (2012).
6. Mitchell and Woodman (2010).
7. See Black *et al.* (2005) for an overview of new governance approaches to regulation

8. OECD (1995); Baldwin (1997); Gunningham *et al.* (1999); Better Regulation Task Force (2000).
9. Gouldson and Murphy (1998); Andersen (1994).
10. Haigh and Irwin (1990).
11. For a discussion of this in the case of New Zealand's Resource Management Act, see OECD (1996).
12. Coglianese (2009).
13. Scholtz (1984).
14. Based on Braithwaite (2008).
15. ENTEC (2003); Amodu (2008).
16. Fresh Minds (2009).
17. BRE (2009).
18. Harris (2002).
19. Vickers *et al.* (2005).
20. Petts *et al.* (1999).
21. Vickers *et al.* (2005).
22. Petts (2000).
23. Baldwin and Black (2008).
24. Haines (1997; 2011) criticizes response regulation from a dual economy perspective: it may be feasible for managing a small number of large organizations but regulators cannot be expected to engage in iterated encounters with a multitude of small businesses.
25. The New Zealand Productivity Commission (2014) reports this to be an issue in New Zealand because of the big step up from low level enforcement tools to the next option of taking a prosecution.
26. Braithwaite (2008), Chapter 4.
27. Black and Baldwin (2010), p. 181.
28. Baldwin (2010), p.6
29. Rumsfeld (2002).
30. Based on Nemetz (2013), p.186.
31. Nemetz (2013), pp. 194–5.
32. See Baldwin (2010), p. 6 for a discussion of this in the case of the UK.
33. For example, see Perrow (1984; 2007).
34. Black (2008).
35. Wiener and Rogers (2002).

36. See de Freitas and Perry (2012), Chapter 4 for further discussion.

37. Braithwaite and Drahos (2000) describe consultants as "model mercenaries" because of their tendency to favor dispensing a limited range of standardized solutions using models that are abstracted from specific practices so as to facilitate the ease of diffusion. The outcome has been labeled "institutional isomorphism" where individual organizations are encouraged to act in the same ways.

38. Something of this response was, for example, identified in a study of the efforts to encourage participation in integrated pollution control in England and Wales—see Murphy and Gouldson (2000).

39. Coglianese and Mendelson (2010).

40. Krut and Gleckman (1998).

41. ISO (2011).

42. Gunningham *et al.* (2004), p. 184.

43. Black (2014).

44. Driesen (2010).

45. Stavins (2003).

46. A full discussion of the varieties of economic instrument can be found in de Freitas and Perry (2012).

47. Driesen and Ghosh (2005).

CHAPTER 3

Information as Regulation

There is a longstanding interest in the possibility of using information sharing as a basis for regulation. The insight obtained from company disclosures can empower the public to evaluate the performance of individual businesses and make businesses more aware of their own performance than where information is kept in-house or not gathered at all. Through these impacts, information sharing has been referred to as informal regulation to reflect how public pressure rather than command and control exercised by a public agency can bring a change of business behavior.[1] Recent developments appear to have strengthened the case for informal regulation with modern information technology enabling greater transparency in the environmental performance of business and in facilitating environmental activism across the globe. The impact is partly voluntary as organizations take advantage of the increased ability to monitor and communicate information and partly a reaction to the growth in environmental campaign groups that makes it harder for organizations to hide their environmental performance. The technological capacity to share information continues to grow, suggesting that adjustment to a new era of transparency is still unfolding. In line with these developments, "radical new transparency" has been identified as one of the three defining characteristics of the new environmentalism that is driving pressure for more sustainable forms of economic development.[2]

One consequence of the new transparency is that a company's social and environmental impact is now less likely to go unnoticed today than previously it may have been. This is seen with the development of information sharing projects such as the GoodGuide (Box 3.1), which seem to confirm the claim that if you do not make information about your supply chain publicly available the chances are that others will do it for you.[3] The impact of radical transparency is said, for example, to be behind

Box 3.1 The GoodGuide

The GoodGuide (www.goodguide.com) is an online database of qualified information about the health, environmental, and social impact
of 65,000 common products. GoodGuide was founded in 2007 by
Dara O'Rourke, professor of environmental and labor policy at the
University of California, Berkeley. It uses a team of scientists and tech-
nologists to vet products in four categories: food, toys, personal care,
and household products. Each of these products is rated and ranked
on numerous criteria, ranging from the harmfulness of its ingredients
to its manufacturer's record on working conditions, diversity, and reporting. The information is accessible via a website or an iPhone application, which can be used to scan the barcode of an item in the shop
for instant feedback.

the speed with which global food companies such as Kraft, Nabisco, and
Nestlé reduced their use of trans fats in the face of health risk concerns.
This is certainly a contrast to an earlier time and the reaction of tobacco
companies to scientific evidence of the dangers of smoking. More directly connected to sustainability, the *Toxics Release Inventory* (TRI) in the
United States is widely cited as an example of the ability of information
transparency to pressure organizations into modifying their activities. The
Environmental Protection Agency administers the TRI and is reported as
regarding the program as one of the most effective environmental initiatives ever undertaken in the United States.[4] Nonetheless questions remain
about the particular achievements of the TRI and the larger potential of
information sharing to be a form of regulation.

The chapter continues by discussing the debate around environmental
reporting and the case for mandatory reporting. This leads on to the out-
line of a framework that can be used to guide the design of information-
based regulation that recognizes various ways that information can bring
change and various degrees to which information can be shared. The experience of the TRI is then considered in the light of this framework.
Finally, the use of environmental labels as another form of information-
based regulation is discussed.

Environmental Reporting

The number of companies producing some form of environmental or broader sustainability report has grown internationally since the 1990s. In broad terms, this is being viewed as a sign that more and more companies are accepting a need to demonstrate their obligation to government, their consumers, and the larger public to be accountable for the environmental and social impacts of their business.[5] The trend continues to be upward in terms of the number of companies releasing such reports but with reporting to remain mainly a feature of a country's largest companies and in most countries for fewer than 50 percent of the largest companies to be regular reporters. Along with the growth of reporting the establishment of the Global Reporting Initiative (GRI) has helped to maintain the value of reporting.

The GRI is now an UN-linked initiative, providing guidelines for environmental, social, and sustainability reporting that aim to give confidence in the content of individual reports.[6] GRI guidelines contain principles and guidance on content, quality, and report boundaries with the aim of making reports a reliable indicator of a company's performance rather than simply being a selective summary of what a company wishes to report about itself. These guidelines, in their fourth edition in 2014, attempt to offer a means of making reports more standardized and comparable across organizations by specifying standard disclosures and recommended ways of reporting performance. As well organizations can have their reports audited against GRI guidelines and lodge their compliant report with the GRI who make it available through their website.

The growth of reporting and large number of organizations submitting reports to the GRI database suggest evidence of business being willing voluntarily to demonstrate their willingness to be accountable for more than their financial performance. In addition, there has been a growth of indices and rankings that make judgments about the sustainability and social responsibility of organizations and for which reporting is one source of evidence used to compile their rankings.[7] Two reasons to doubt that reporting in itself signifies a shift in business behavior have been proposed by a longtime observer of corporate reporting trends.[8] First, it remains confined to a small minority of businesses even among multinational corporations. Second, reporting is usually used as an opportunity to suggest a positive image of the organization's activities and as such they are essentially one-sided and incomplete documents. Voluntary reporting is being used by companies partly to help shape what society thinks are a company's responsibilities so as to keep their accountability to matters they feel able to manage. The question is asked, therefore, whether environmental and sustainability reporting should become compulsory in the same way that companies are required to report their financial performance.

There have already been moves to make the disclosure of environmental information compulsory.[9] For example, in the United States, the Securities and Exchange Commission requires that companies disclose how compliance with environmental regulations may affect the company's financial performance, to indicate whether it is subject to any legal action arising under environmental laws and to declare any environmental matters that could have a bearing on a company's operations and performance. In France and Spain, companies have been required to include information about their social and environmental impacts within their annual reports. Generally, compliance with these requirements in Europe has been low with the bodies responsible for monitoring and enforcing compliance facing a number of challenges in improving the situation. Low cooperation suggests that demands for environmental reporting should be based on a clear understanding of the costs and benefits of environmental disclosure.

A Framework for Information-Based Regulation

A general justification for information-based regulation is that information enables people to make informed decisions. Information sharing is thus sometimes presented as a form of market-based regulation where the emphasis is on reducing "market friction." Market mechanisms assume that decision makers are well informed about the costs and benefits of their decisions. In this sense, requiring or encouraging the disclosure of information reduces market friction. Information disclosure has thus been seen as the "third wave" of environmental policy making (after command and control and market-based instruments) because it is thought that many environmental problems can be reduced through increased awareness of their existence and because the costs of providing, processing, and disseminating relevant information have been changing.[10] Nonetheless, the use of information as a basis for regulation needs to be informed by an understanding of how it can change business behavior and what forms of information sharing are needed to bring the change in behavior. In addition, consideration needs to be given to the costs of collecting and reporting performance data.

When dealing with the release of "raw data," such as volumes of toxic materials emitted, volumes of waste generated, or proportion of waste recycled, there are three further and more specific justifications for information sharing beyond the general claim of eliminating market friction, each of which suggests a potential set of benefits.[11]

- *Normative*: the public has a "right to know" about the risks created by the activities of business and other entities that receive legal and other privileges bestowed by public agencies. This right to know is part of the "license to operate" that enables citizens to make informed decisions about the risks to which they are potentially exposed.
- *Substantive*: the release of data has the potential to produce new insights and understanding of environmental problems and how to remedy them. This may occur internally within the organizations disclosing information as the process for collecting data encourages thinking about processes for reducing adverse impacts. Externally, sharing information with government agencies may enable the better design of public programs, for example, by understanding where to focus improvement efforts.
- *Instrumental*: disclosure can "shock and shame" poor performers into taking action. The release of risk and impact data shocks citizens, the media, agencies, and markets who become external sources of pressure on organizations. In turn, companies feel a sense of shame that drives them to initiate change.

Against these possible reasons, there are costs associated with public disclosure. Most obviously, there is a cost in collecting and reporting information, because this may require that an organization invests in monitoring and data recording equipment. Allowing the use of proxy measures (for example, allowing emissions to be inferred from the volume of inputs utilized) can reduce costs but lessen the reliability of the data. Two more complex costs should also be recognized.

- Public disclosure brings a risk of public perception determining environmental standards or at least gaining more influence at the cost of public agency determination of standards and priorities. This cost increases according to the extent to which public opinion is dominated by sectional interests with priorities informed by incomplete, biased, or inaccurate understanding. The general experience of public participation is that sensitivity to perceived risk rather than real risk influences community activism.
- Public disclosure programs generally have a particular public in mind when encouraging information release such as those residing within a particular administrative area or in proximity to a source of pollution. In practice, it can be difficult to restrict access to publicly disclosed information or the purpose to which it is put. An extreme possibility, for example, is that information on toxic chemicals or radioactive substances directs terrorists to potential targets or bomb-making materials.

Combining benefit and cost considerations, a number of design principles give most prospect of information disclosure motivating a change in business behavior.

- The disclosure program must require the collection of new data that gives business managers a clear sense of what to target and an ability to measure improvement against the investment made. Managers are motivated when they have new information to act upon and that enables progress to be monitored.

- Information must empower communities if it is going to increase the pressure on organizations to invest in environmental improvement. Local communities need to be able to use their greater understanding of environmental risks in accessible and significant forms of dialog with industry and public agency staff. At present, resource consent processes are the main opportunity for public participation. Such processes tend to be a complex, drawn out and demanding for community groups to sustain involvement in. Public disclosure needs guidance from a better understanding than currently exists of the channels through which communities can affect industry behavior.

- The costs of collecting data, actual or perceived, are a potential source of industry resistance to disclosure programs. Additional costs are involved if information must be released to public agencies and the community, but the main costs arise from the collection of data rather than its dissemination. Further insight is needed into the costs of data collection to understand the factors that contribute to higher costs and how the use of information technology may help to reduce them.

- Data quality is critical to the effectiveness of disclosure. The key challenge is that disclosure tends to release only part of the information needed for a complete risk assessment. Fragmentary information combined with established perceptions of risk can lead the public to over- or under-react to information compared with what a full technical assessment of the risk might suggest is justified. This context can strain the credibility of disclosure where NGOs, the media, and companies make competing claims over the significance of the fragment of the risk assessment that is disclosed.

- Risks associated with the unintended use of data need to be managed. Following the September 11 terrorist attacks in the United States, Environmental Protection Agency of that country produced some guidelines to help reduce the usefulness of environmental disclosure data to criminals. These include taking note of the ability to combine data with other information to create more insight into a plant and controlling the release of sensitive information.

Given the need to balance benefits and costs, four levels of disclosure have been identified from information capture without public disclosure (level one) to full disclosure (level four) (Figure 3.1). The first level merely encourages or requires organizations to collect environmental information without any need to release this data to any external agency or person. This is effectively what occurs when organizations are required to have

Figure 3.1 A framework for designing information-based regulation[12]

Benefit/ cost of the disclosure	Level of disclosure			
	1. Firm only	2. Firm-government	3. Community disclosure	4. Full disclosure
Benefits	BN N/A BS Possible BI Possible	BN N/A BS Possible BI Unlikely change over other forms of regulation	BN Possible BS Possible if community input accepted BI Possible if disclosure is perceived as a threat threat and is used by community activists to shame a firm/industry	BN Contested need for a right to know BS Possible if third parties add new insight BI Possible if disclosure is perceived as a threat and is used by activists to shame a firm/industry
Costs	C1	C2	C3 Risk of misinformed use varies with a firm's ability to control use of data	C4 Uncertain outcomes but generally low ability to maintain control of data

Table scores

Benefits: BN. Normative "right to know" exercised; BS. Substantive benefits obtained as information generates new insights; BI. Instrumental benefit from "shock and shame" response.
Costs: C1. Collection costs only C2. Collection and reporting costs; C3. Collection and reporting costs and risk of misinformed use; C4. Collection and reporting costs and risk of misinformed and unwanted use;

a certified environmental management system (EMS) program such as ISO14001 (see Chapter 2 and metaregulation). Such programs require the collection of monitoring information but do not require public disclosure. Between this level and full disclosure, information is shared with a selected audience that as a minimum (level two) includes public agencies. Beyond this, selective disclosure may be achieved through establishing community liaison committees, open days, newsletters, and through reporting in mandatory documents such as company annual reports.

The Toxics Release Inventory

As noted above, the Toxics Release Inventory (TRI) in the United States is the most recognized and influential information disclosure program used by environmental managers. Its success, for example, led the OECD (1997) to recommend that member nations introduce similar pollutant release and transfer registers to provide a public database of industrial releases to air, water, and soil and of waste transported to treatment and disposal sites. The TRI itself was one of the responses to the devastating chemical accident at the Union Carbide plant in Bhopal, India, in 1984 (another response being the chemical industry's self-regulation program Responsible Care, see Chapter 1). The TRI was intended originally as a mechanism for improving the understanding of potential risks from industrial facilities. Subsequent experience indicated that reported toxic releases were reducing with a drop of 46 percent over the first 11 years of disclosure. With this evidence of the apparent power of transparency, the program's coverage has expanded and increased efforts made to release information in ways that community groups and individuals can make use of to monitor the use of toxic chemicals in their locality. At the same time, investigation of the TRI and other information sharing initiatives indicates that it is important to recognize that multiple influences are frequently at work, some of which may have nothing to do with increased transparency.

Various studies have suggested that the TRI encouraged instrumental pressure on the users of toxic chemicals that resulted in the drop in reported emission.[13] For example, one study detected a link between movements in stock prices and the release of emissions data through the TRI:

high reported emissions resulted in high falls in the value of the reporting entities shares.[14] The researchers in this case added a note of caution to their findings, including that they were unable to determine whether share traders were reacting to other aspects of the company rather than the TRI data, such as evidence of production inefficiency. There is reason to expect that this may be the case since high emissions may be associated with the use of out-of-date technology, with the use of old technology being a sign of business under performance.

In practice, claims that the TRI itself was a cause of change tend to rely on research evidence that assumes the only reason for a change in the reported emissions is the requirement for public disclosure. This can overlook how companies may be responding to other regulation affecting the use of certain chemicals and how market factors may influence production activity and reported emissions. A case study of the primary aluminum industry shows both these influences to have played a big part in reported emissions levels.[15] That research also finds evidence of underreporting, low levels of compliance, and of how variation in reported levels can reflect changes in the estimation methods and classification systems employed. This study does not rule out entirely that instrumental influences may have also contributed to emission reductions, but it does indicate that any such influence cannot be inferred simply by examining changes in reported emission levels.

In the case of the aluminum industry, the act of annually gathering and reporting emissions data in itself appears to have encouraged a range of responses others than those intended. The positive interpretation of the TRI assumes that the reported data accurately measure actual emissions: this is a prerequisite for firms to find them of substantive benefit and for them to be concerned about the impression created by the data. Unless the emissions are simple to measure, it takes strict enforcement of reporting requirements via regular site visits and independent third-party auditing to ensure good quality data are reported. In circumstances where this is not occurring, it appears firms will exploit the flexibility allowed within reporting requirements to present their activity in the most favorable light. Rather than offering a self-managing form of regulation, information-based regulation like the TRI has chance to work only if there is intensive administration and strict rules to ensure data returns are reliable and comprehensive. This has not been part of the regulation, which helps to explain why a survey of 1,000 facilities covered by TRI reporting requirements found it to be having little influence in motivating pollution reduction.[16] Similarly, a Canadian study of the equivalent to the TRI in that country (the National Pollution Release Inventory) found that the emissions reductions identified through the disclosure were mainly associated with a few polluters responding to direct regulation of the pollution involved.[17]

As to the costs associated with the TRI, the EPA has identified a range of issues that complicate the interpretation of reported emissions and which run the risk of leading to inappropriate interpretations of what the data imply for public safety and the quality of the environment.[18] The EPA gives seven reasons for caution in the use of their emissions data: the relative toxicity such that raw volumes are a poor indicator when used to compare chemicals of differing risk; the persistence of the chemical in the environment; the form in which the chemical is released, which impacts the routes of exposure such as inhalation, ingestion, and absorption; the potential for bioconcentration in the food chain; the type of disposal or release (whether to air, water, soil, or underground injection); the type of off-site facility receiving the chemical; the efficiency of waste management practices; and the on-site waste management of the toxic chemical.

An examination of three post-TRI disclosure programs in the United States, underlines the point that disclosure programs need to have a clear purpose and be based on information sharing mechanisms that can fulfill that purpose.[19] Information disclosure on its own may not be sufficient to bring changes in behavior and contrawise in some circumstances simply requiring organizations to collect data can bring improvement. Consequently, while a country such as New Zealand has made little use of public disclosure as an environmental management tool against the recommendations made by the OECD,[20] it is evident that the power of information disclosure is less than is frequently supposed, although this does not negate the case for requiring more disclosure as part of the "right to know."

Environmental Labels

The TRI requires the release of raw performance data. In theory, this has the advantage of providing an objective assessment of an organization's performance and of allowing communities to better understand the risks to which they are exposed. A limitation is that it is hard to prevent manipulation of the reporting and raw data may require expert interpretation to gauge the significance of what is reported. Imposing strict rules on the release of data is an option along with requirements for organizations to declare how measurement is conducted and to demonstrate that their measurement is appropriate to their situation. This possibility needs to be balanced against the risks that requiring more detail to be reported will result in environmental reports becoming complex and ultimately hard to penetrate. The idea of producing "chapter and verse" seems sensible in theory, but in practice may result in environmental reports that are hard for most people to understand and that can simply act to help companies defend their actions. A few key statistics are potentially easier to grasp and harder to defend than where companies are required to submit extended information declarations. The use of environmental performance labels, or as they are more generally known, *ecolabels* is one application of the perspective that requiring the release of a few key performance measures is likely to be more effective than extended data releases.

Product labeling to encourage adherence to particular production standards has a long history associated with regional food and beverage specialities. The role of this labeling is to protect localized business clusters from competition, whereas environmental labeling aims to encourage competition based on environmental performance. Nonetheless, it is worth recognizing some of the issues with regional food labels, because they can arise with environmental labeling too (Box 3.2).

Ecolabel schemes allow the use of a licensed logo on products that have passed preset environmental performance criteria. Following the introduction of the Blue Angel mark in Germany in 1977, such labeling schemes have been introduced in most OECD countries. Certification is generally based on a *life cycle assessment* (LCA) of the product's impact on the environment from design to disposal. These schemes partly came about in response to the growth of "green advertising" where producers

Box 3.2 Product Labeling to Recognize Regional Uniqueness[21]

The French *appellation d'origine controlee* (AOC) is the oldest form of regional product labeling in Europe and is regarded as the strictest of its kind. AOC labels are controlled by a government agency and give assurance of the territorial origin and conformance to the precise production and processing methods that guarantee a distinctive character. The system is based on *terroir* which, translated crudely, refers to how production in specific places results in unique product qualities derived from specific environmental conditions and methods of production perfected and handed down over many generations. Originally applied mainly to wine and spirits, claims of *terroir* are now attached to a growing range of land-based products, including cheese and meats.

AOCs are credited with helping to maintain agricultural profitability in areas that are marginal for industrial farming methods. Natural environmental qualities are given most attention in the decision to award an AOC, but this does not mean that production is beneficial for the environment. It may, for example, limit the varieties of crop planted. It may help preserve traditional hillside terraces that are a form of erosion control, but this means a modified rather than a natural environment is protected. The geographical boundaries within which *terroir* may be claimed respect historical associations, which may have little regard to ecological transitions. Lobbying over boundary changes goes on with an increasing range of stakeholders frequently getting involved, including tourism and rural development interests that see economic opportunity in the award of an AOC. Tasting panels set up to monitor product conformance are guided by political as well as gastronomic considerations.

made unsubstantiated claims about the environmental performance of their goods. Labels aim to provide some certainty and standardization to the claim of being "good for the environment." Originally, the thinking in Europe was that single national schemes should be encouraged to ensure their credibility, but it now tends to be thought that having rival schemes can encourage innovation in product assessment techniques and strengthen efforts to maintain interest in the programs.[22] More recently, a consensus has been reached that environmental labels should be based on a LCA of the product's impact on the environment from design to disposal, or sometimes referred to as cradle-to-grave. This is to prevent a situation where industry groups design labels around a single criterion that companies are comfortable to compete over. For example, in Europe, an association of light bulb manufacturers reportedly made their involvement in the development of a label conditional on the criteria being restricted to energy efficiency.[23] Life cycle analysis guards against labeling on the basis of selective performance measures, but it is far from a perfect tool for gauging the relative environmental impacts of different products or services (Box 3.3).

Box 3.3 The Limits of Life Cycle Analysis[24]

LCA aims to identify environmental impacts associated with the creation, use, and disposal of a product. The value and credibility of any LCA depends on the quality of data on which it is based. An accurate LCA requires that direct as well as indirect impacts are measured. This is not easy. Impacts of the same product or process will vary according to the environmental and regulatory conditions encountered. The importance and severity of environmental impacts often depends upon local conditions, which vary within and between countries and which can change over time. One option is to use standardized impact data for an average product made in and disposed of in an average environment, but such approximation can make LCA results unreliable. Moreover, the output of a LCA is merely a recommendation of the least environmentally damaging option. The recommended option may still result in serious impacts on the environment through the cumulative effects of mass consumption. LCA is consistent with a cradle-to-grave approach that accepts a need for waste and end-of-life disposal, as compared with a "cradle-to-cradle" or ecoeffective approach that aims to exclude harmful environmental impacts from industrial systems.

The environmental certification of organizations is another form of labeling. This kind of certification is directed at business managers, because it is the administrative routines and structures of organizations that are assessed rather than actual environmental standards and performance. ISO14001 has become the internationally most important standard for EMSs (see Chapter 2). As a certified scheme, ISO14001 provides an opportunity for industry to establish an EMS that is verified against an external standard and accredited by an independent agency (although ISO regulations do permit self-certification, most companies use external auditors).

Ideally, certification is a labeling scheme and an instrument that guides improvement effort within an organization. The risk is that "the certificates of compliance are often pinned to the wall and subsequently forgotten about until the auditors are due again."[25] In this regard, it has been argued that five elements are required of an EMS before they should be regarded as a regulatory instrument.[26]

- Compliance requirements to ensure certificates are awarded to organizations that comply with all other forms of environmental regulation.
- There is a demonstration of actual improvements in environmental performance, rather than just a need to demonstrate that there are processes to ensure that continual improvement of the management system occurs.
- There is a third-party verification of the audit conducted that judges whether the organization is compliant to the EMS.
- The EMS requires the public reporting of information relating to the organization's environmental impacts and performance.
- There is opportunity for outside participation in the verification of an organization's environmental performance and targets.

As discussed in the context of the possibility of ISO14001 being used as a form of metaregulation (Chapter 2), these components are missing. Nonetheless, and as reflected in the uptake of ISO14001 in newly industrializing economies, there is value in encouraging a systematic approach to environmental management.[27]

Do Labels Work?

Interest in labeling programs appears to have peaked. In most countries, product labeling schemes have remained confined to a few product areas such as detergents, paints, and toiletry items. The diffusion of labeling reflects conditions prevailing within industries such as the ease of satisfying criteria, the degree of consumer awareness and interest and the ease of getting business support for a label scheme.[28] Depending on the balance of these influences, business populations attached to individual industries have been identified as responding in different ways.

- Cooperation has arisen where industry participants perceive that addressing an environmental challenge is supportive of the industry's preferred technology. This can be because the environmental concerns are focused on one aspect of the industry's product rather than fundamentally challenging current business practice. For example, the paint and varnish industry has accepted the need to reduce volatile organic compounds partly because this did not conflict with other competitive strategies individual firms wish to deploy.
- Resistance to an ecolabel has arisen where industry participants share a common view that labeling criteria would be hard to achieve and of limited interest to consumers. The manufacture of hairsprays was identified as fitting this situation.
- Industry division is a third possible response where some businesses align themselves to a labeling scheme and others stay outside. The laundry detergent industry was identified as an example with businesses differentiated according to their assessment of the marketing potential of "green" detergent.

The regulatory efficiency of labeling schemes versus other tools remains largely unexplored. A study of energy efficiency labeling suggests that such labels are effective in making consumers more sensitive to energy price changes than otherwise they would be. For example, the perceived success of energy performance labeling has led to a joint New Zealand–Australia Equipment Energy Efficiency (E3) Program that since 2006 has been developing mandatory energy efficiency labels and performance standards for a range of commonly used electrical residential, commercial, and industrial products. New Zealand also encourages voluntary product endorsement through the "energy star" scheme that was first developed by the United States Department of Energy to encourage consumers to purchase more efficient products.

Traceability

Increased capacity for connectivity is certainly a feature of the IT-enabled world that is opening business activity to higher levels of scrutiny than in the past. This is reflected in the development of systems for product *traceability* back to the suppliers of the raw material on which a product is based. This is an area which some companies are exploiting for business advantage. Icebreaker is a New Zealand example that has gained international attention.[29] Buyers of new Icebreaker clothes are given a reference number or "baacode" with a garment that enables them to view online the farm where the merino wool was grown. Links include a video of farmer Ray Anderson who tells how his family has run Branch Creek station for more than 100 years. Icebreaker says they persisted with the expensive and technically challenging project because a growing number of consumers demand proof of a company's commitment to the environment before they are prepared to buy.

Traceability is a form of transparency that many producers who are confident of their environmental performance are seeking to earn an advantage from. Use of the new capacity for tracking back to upstream suppliers is spreading, helped by it being a tool for increasing supply chain efficiencies as well as for enabling traceability and demonstrating environmental responsibility. In New Zealand, for example, the National Animal Identification and Traceability (NAIT) standard makes radio-frequency identification tags mandatory on all beef cattle from October 2011 with the tag following the meat recovered from the animal as part of food safety management.

Chapter Summary

Information disclosure programs need to have a clear purpose and need to be based on information sharing mechanisms that will fulfill that purpose. Information disclosure on its own may not be sufficient to bring changes in behavior and contrawise in some circumstances simply requiring organizations to collect data can bring improvement.

Environmental information can be complex and open to alternative interpretations. This can make it important that there are intermediary agencies in existence to process raw information into more useable and insightful forms. But it also seems that organizations are developing increased sensitivity to the risk of being exposed as a poor performer. One reason for this is that competitors may include responsible companies who are choosing to harness the power of transparency, fostering innovation, customer loyalty, and brand awareness.

Key Concepts

Ecolabel: third-party certificate endorsing an aspect of a product's or service's environmental performance.

Environmental reporting: a means for organizations to communicate environmentally relevant information about their activities to people and agencies outside their organization, voluntarily or as required by regulation.

Instrumental: as a reason for information sharing, improvement in environmental performance due to public pressure also referred to as "shock and shame."

Life cycle assessment: a complete audit of the environmental impacts of all the products and services associated with the product or service being assessed, including the impacts associated with the use and end-of-life disposal.

Normative: as a reason for information sharing, the "right to know" is the principle that in open societies the public have a right to information as to how the actions of other parties may be exposing them to risks.

Substantive: as a reason for information sharing, the additional insight obtained into managing environmental impacts.

Toxics Release Inventory: a program requiring users of designated toxic chemicals in the United States to release information about the volumes and type of chemicals used.

Traceability: ability to track products back to the source of the raw material on which the product is based.

Endnotes

1. Pargal and Wheeler (1996).
2. Laszlo and Zhexembayeva (2011); de Freitas and Perry (2012).
3. Tyrrell (2010).
4. Graham and Miller (2001).
5. To track trends in environmental reporting see the KPMG International Survey of Corporate Responsibility 2013 and earlier versions of this survey that started in 1997. Available from http://www.kpmg .com/global/en/issuesandinsights/articlespublications/corporate-responsibility/pages/default.aspx. For commentary on environmental and social responsibility reporting see Kolk (2008); White (2009); Gray and Herremans (2012).
6. www.globalreporting.org
7. Examples are the Dow Jones Sustainbility Index and the FTSE 4Good index.
8. Gray and Herremans (2012), p. 411.
9. See Cho *et al.* (2012).
10. Tietenberg (1998).
11. This discussion draws on Stephan (2002) and Beierle (2003).
12. Table based on information in Beierle (2003).
13. For example, see Konar and Cohen (1997); Lynn and Kartez (1997); Fung and O'Rourke (2000).
14. Konar and Cohen (1997).
15. Koehler and Spengler (2007).
16. Stephan *et al.* (2005).
17. Harrison and Antweiler (2001).

18. Nemetz (2013) and for information on the use of the Toxics release Inventory, see EPA (2013) and http://toxmap.nlm.nih.gov/toxmap/faq/toxics-release-inventory-tri/
19. Beierle (2003).
20. OECD (2007: 173).
21. This box draws on material in Barham (2003).
22. Sterner (2003).
23. West (1995).
24. For a critique of life cycle analysis, see Arnold (1995).
25. Welford (1995), p. 79.
26. Krut and Gleckman (1998).
27. For a positive account of ISO14001, see Hillary (2000) and for its connection to total responsibility management, see Waddock and Bodwell (2007); Gorenak and Bobek (2010).
28. Nadaï (1999).
29. Fifield (2010).

CHAPTER 4

Emission Trading

Economic or market-based instruments aim to give the greatest incentive to mitigate environmental impacts to organizations that are able to make change at least cost. If this is achieved, it should mean that the environment is protected at least overall cost to society. This quality of economic instruments is frequently contrasted with regulatory approaches that seek to equalize the environmental standards adhered to across all organizations. Rather than equalizing the standard attained by each individual organization, economic instruments focus on the overall level of environmental performance for an economy as a whole and seek to equalize the expenditure regulated organizations must make for this desired level of environmental protection to be obtained. The underlying justification is that it is not necessary to force all polluters to stop polluting as long as there are some who are able to greatly reduce their environmental impacts so that pollution as a whole goes down.

Emissions trading became the policy option of choice for addressing *greenhouse gas emissions* largely through the advocacy of U.S. negotiators during the discussions that led to the 1997 *Kyoto Protocol* to the Framework Convention on Climate Change.[1] This agreement included within it a *Clean Development Mechanism* (CDM) that allowed project developers in signatory countries to earn pollution reduction credits through emission reducing projects located in developing countries. The underlying perspective was that since it does not matter where reductions in greenhouse gases occur, it made economic sense to allow reductions to come from low-income countries even though these countries were not subject to the emission limitations imposed by the Kyoto Protocol. Having established the CDM, signatory nations then put in place domestic policies that could be integrated with the globalized environmental benefit trading it allowed. Consequently, having initially opposed emissions trading as a policy approach, the European Union introduced the first mandatory emissions trading scheme for controlling greenhouse gas emissions—the EU Emissions Trading Scheme (ETS).

This chapter continues by providing the background theory supporting emission trading. It then considers the case of sulfur dioxide trading in the United States, which was used in the context of a policy initiative to reduce the generation of acid rain from power station emissions. Widely seen as a successful use of emission trading, questions have been raised about the actual role played by emissions trading in helping United States manage its acid rain problem. This case is linked to the more recent experience of using emission trading to control greenhouse gas emissions. The role of offsetting is then explained with consideration of the case for tightening the circumstances where it should be allowed as part of emission trading policy.

Emissions Trading Theory

The theory behind *tradable or transferable permits* is that they can achieve the same reduction in environmental damage as command and control regulation without needing to be concerned with how individual organizations respond to the need to achieve an overall reduction in pollution. Rather regulatory agencies can leave it to polluters themselves to work out who will make the cutbacks in pollution. Moreover, *emission trading* is thought to offer more certainty that pollution reduction targets will be met than would the use of environmental taxes. To explain how emission trading is thought to improve on these other regulatory options, this section starts by explaining how emission trading avoids the main drawback of using environmental taxes.

The Limitations of Environmental Taxes

Environment charges aim to reduce the level of environmental impact from a specific activity by levying a fee or tax per unit of that activity. The charge reduces as the level of activity goes down. In theory, this means that those subject to a charge have an incentive to reduce their activity or to take mitigation measures. For the individual polluter, the strength of the incentive to contribute less pollution is determined by the cost of taking action. So, if the charge to pollute was going to be $500, for example, there is cost-saving reason to spend $499 on avoiding the tax but not to address environmental impacts if this were to cost $501. To achieve the purpose of reducing environmental damage, therefore, the level at which the charge is set is critical to its effectiveness. The ideal environmental charge would result in each polluter paying an amount equal to the individual incremental damage of their pollution. These are sometimes referred to as true *Pigovian taxes* after the economist Pigou who is credited with originating the idea. So, for example, if burning a liter of petrol to fuel a car creates $1 of environmental damage the tax should be set at $1 per liter of petrol. In practice, precise costing of environmental damage is not possible.

The idea that damage should be paid for inspires the use of charges as a signal to polluters about society's wish for a change in behavior even if it is unlikely to achieve a true Pigovian correction. Taxes and charges can provide a strong economic incentive to invest in environmental measures. Nonetheless, practical issues tend to limit the ability to rely on environmental taxes as a basis for environmental regulation.

- With an environmental tax, organizations face a double financial burden as the tax payable is high when the environmental mitigation costs are likely to be high too. A large tax bill implies that costly remedial measures are needed to get the bill down. Allowing abatement expenditure to offset tax payments or levying a tax only on impacts above a specified level are possible ways of reducing this dilemma. Modifications imply the need for regulatory administration, highlighting how charges can be used in conjunction but not in place of "command and control."
- Setting the level of the tax or charge is a significant challenge if the intention is to encourage a significant reduction in environmental damage. "Trial and error" may be the only option, adjusting the tax according to observed changes in environmental impact. A possibility is to base the charge or tax on a measurable input that has some relationship with

the environmental impact (for example, using expenditure on fertilizer as a proxy for the impact of farming on the nutrient loading of waterways) or to link tax levels to typical abatement costs.

- Charges may not give sufficient control where it is important to keep environmental impacts within a critical threshold. The uncertainty of what, if any reduction in damaging activity is produced by a charge means that there is insufficient control. Taxes and charges are practical where it is sufficient merely to signal that there are environmental costs rather than to attain a precise level of control.

How Emission Trading Works

Under an *emission trading* or tradable permit scheme, an allowable overall level of pollution is established and allocated among firms in the form of permits. Organizations that keep their environmental impacts below their allotted level may sell their surplus permits to other firms or use them to offset impacts generated by other parts of their organization that are beyond the permitted level. A cap on the overall level of emissions determines the volume of permits allocated. Hence, this approach is sometimes called "cap and trade."

The permit approach can be applied to pollution control problems as well as to the allocation of an environmental resource among users where the resulting instrument is typically known as an *individual transferable quota* (ITQ). Indeed, the use of ITQ's to manage inshore fisheries is one of the main examples of the sustained use of tradable permits (Box 4.1). Whatever the form taken, tradable permits in effect allocate ownership rights to some aspect of the environment. These rights give a share of the assimilative capacity of the environment (as assessed by environmental managers), such as the right to emit pollutants into the atmosphere, or a right (or ITQ) to use a share of an ecosystem such as a fishery. This apportionment of ownership rights has been likened to a continuation of the historic process of "enclosure."[2] Some view enclosure (private ownership) as a necessary starting point for good environmental behavior assuming that owners are motivated to look after their resources. This can overlook that

Box 4.1 Individual Transferable Quotas and Fisheries Management[3]

An individual transferable quota scheme was introduced for fishing in New Zealand's coastal waters in 1986. It responded to evidence that fish stocks were declining and estimates that the full-time inshore fishing fleet was almost double the size of that justified by the size of the fishery. At the time, the use of ITQ was credited with giving New Zealand the most advanced fisheries quota system in the world. Under the scheme, individual fish species are designated a total allowable catch (which varies according to an assessment of the state of the fish stock) which is allocated, at no cost to the individual fishers receiving the initial quota distribution according to the historic participation in the fishery. Purchasing or leasing individual transferable quotas is then allowed. More than 30 of the commercially most important fish species are now controlled through the quota system. As well, the quota system permits the Government to set restrictions over the fishing methods, timing of activity, and precise areas fished.

In theory, transferability of quota enables the most efficient operators to accumulate quota from less-efficient operators. Alongside the setting of a total allowable catch, this should encourage the conservation of fish stocks, given that quota holders gain an incentive to protect the long-term value of their quota. This ideal outcome relies on the accurate setting of the total allowable catch, acceptance of that limit, and the removal of any motivation to exceed the quota limit to maintain a minimum short-term return on the quota investment.

Overfishing of quota limits, misrepresenting catch data, catching fish for which quota is not held, and overfishing of the more accessible fishing grounds are known problems. Fishers have frequently challenged scientific assessments that report a need for reducing quota volumes while environmental groups are concerned that the total allowable commercial catch is based on an assessment of the catch level that can be sustained over ten years rather than setting quota limits year-by-year.

many other management arrangements can work effectively too and that enclosure can conflict with the public access to environmental resources and public interest in how some environmental resources are managed.

Trading of the pollution or ownership rights facilitates economic change (businesses gain an additional incentive to introduce more environmentally friendly methods) and allows new businesses into a sector controlled by the trading scheme (provided there are permits to buy). Transferability also enables those who achieve large reductions in pollutants to sell part of their allocation of permits at a profit to others. Producers should then be motivated to think about their environmental impacts and to search for innovative, low cost ways of reducing them. In the case of transferable quota schemes, individual quota holders are motivated to adhere to sustainable harvesting practices because this protects and potentially enhances the value of the quota rights they hold.

As well as the setting of an initial total limit on the emissions or resource demands, tradable permits differ from environmental taxes in the distribution of the revenue obtained. In a charging system, the revenue is collected by the agency managing the scheme and may or may not be reallocated to addressing the environmental issue. (In a strict Pigovian sense, the revenue raised should not be used to address the environmental impact as the payment of the tax indicates society's acceptance of the damage.) As well, a charging system requires all producers to make a payment unless they have no impacts within the scope of the program. With tradable permits, revenue goes directly to organizations that minimize their pollution (provided surplus permits are sold) and the extent of competition for permits determines how much is paid and the extent to which payment encourages environmental management. Nonetheless, there can be important revenue redistribution implications of emission trading that affect the acceptability of this form of regulation.

The distribution of the economic burden of a trading scheme is affected by the method used for allocating the initial distribution of permits or quota. The government agency designing the scheme must decide whether permits are distributed:

- equally among the potential users
- in proportion to the size of the organizations

- by a lottery that allocates entitlements at random
- by an auction according to the highest bids obtained
- or by some mix of these approaches.

The *grandfathering* principle allocates permits without charge to the recipient according to their historic level of emissions or past use of the resource. It endorses the status quo, defusing some aspects of potential opposition to the introduction of emission trading and for this reason has been the method of initial allocation most frequently used. Grandfathering tends to favor the existing major polluters or largest resource users while creating a barrier for new entrants who must purchase permits from existing holders who received them free of charge. Allocating pollution permits free of charge also has wider implications that some economists suggest can affect the extent to which society as a whole benefits from environmental improvement.[4]

Any form of regulation that imposes higher standards on producers whose output is used by most households (such as power plants, refineries, and transport) tends to be moderately regressive in their impact on the distribution of income. That is, the increase in product and service prices as a consequence of the cost of regulation tends to hurt lower-income groups disproportionately because most of their income is absorbed by expenditure affected by the regulation than is that of wealthy households. This outcome can be exaggerated by the grandfathering of permits. Grandfathering tends to consolidate the position of large incumbents by giving them an additional economic asset in the form of pollution permits. Assuming these incumbents are privately owned, the value of the asset gained is distributed according to the profile of the company's share ownership, which typically is weighted in favor of the most wealthy citizens A study in the United States that assumed carbon emission permits to secure a 15 percent carbon reduction were grandfathered found that the annual real spending power of the lowest income quintile would reduce by $530 while the annual real spending power of the highest income quintile would increase by $1,810.[5] Clearly, this affect is less where utility companies are publicly owned or where a proportion of shares are owned by public interest groups such as sovereign wealth funds.

Auctioning permits can reduce the regressive impact of an emission trading scheme. As well, an auction generates revenue for government that can be returned to households or used for environmental management or other purposes. A mix of grandfathering and auctioning is also possible. A mixed mechanism can also be attractive in allowing the volume of permits to be adjusted according to evidence about the impact of an initial allocation of permits.[6] The responsibility to recognize customary resource entitlements and to protect communities with a particular association with a resource may also need to be considered in the allocation of permits. Connected to this, critics of tradable permit schemes raise questions about the approach to addressing environmental problems through monetary valuation and markets alone.[7]

Experience with Emission Trading

The control of sulfur dioxide (SO_2) emissions from power generation in the United States is frequently the main example given of a successful use of tradable permits. It was developed to serve as a model program to advance the use of market-based environmental regulation and is credited with changing the assessment of at least some parts of the environmental lobby in the United States and of making them keen advocates of emission trading.[8] Responding to a growing acid rain problem, the SO_2 emissions reduction program aimed to cut the annual SO_2 emissions from power plants by 10 million tons under phase one (1995–2000) and by a similar amount in phase two (2000–2010). It sets a cap that demanded a large reduction in emissions, required state-of-the-art continuous emissions monitoring to give all participants certainty in the emissions data informing the scheme's operation, and allowed trading in permits among any party that wished to buy or sell them, including environmentalists seeking to reduce the availability of permits. This brought a high degree of integrity to the program sustaining the confidence of industry to comply with the intentions of the program. The scheme was softened by allowing *offsets* (allowing emissions to be exceeded in some localities); *bubbles* (allowing a group of plants to be treated as one unit) and banking (allowing permits to be saved for future years) and did not seek to be comprehensive of all the pollution for which power plants were responsible.

Phase one targets were achieved, which contributed to a largely positive assessment of the program. Others have pointed out that the program worked in the context of favorable supporting conditions without which it is unclear whether anything like the same impact would have eventuated.[9]

- The cost of abatement technology such as air scrubbers fell significantly after the program started.
- Simultaneous deregulation of the rail industry decreased the cost of freight and increased the commercial availability of low sulfur coal.
- Some states introduced local environmental regulations that added to the pressure on power plants to cut emissions.

Rather than establishing the case for emission trading, the acid rain program can be used to highlight a number of preconditions required for the effective operation of this form of regulation. Above all, there must be a high level of administrative integrity to give participants confidence in the seriousness of the program's intentions and that all participants are behaving according to the trading rules (such as accurately measuring their emissions). The opportunity to engage in trading is a further precondition for success: there must be available technology that polluters are variously positioned to take immediate advantage of. As well, the ideal is to introduce schemes in the context of an operating environment that is broadly in support of the shift to lower emissions without being associated with disruptive changes in market or technology conditions that undermine the assumptions on which the scheme was introduced. A good understanding of the costs of abatement is required too; a requirement that tends to mean emission trading is not suited to managing previously unregulated issues.

To achieve an overall fall in pollution, emission trading occurs within a cap reflected in the volume of permits allocated and that can be reduced over time by program administrators in line with their policy targets. Getting the overall permit allocation right is crucial to the trading incentive. If too many polluters can too easily obtain large amounts of emission rights, then the incentives for abatement are reduced. Even high polluters may need to purchase only a relatively modest volume of permits to keep on polluting while those with excess permits obtain minimal economic benefit from having a surplus of pollution rights. The European Union experienced this with the first phase of its ETS, which is generally recognized to have given away too many tradable permits. A second phase of the program drew on this experience but was then undermined by the global financial crisis and deep recession in several European economies. The knock on effect of the recession was a steep drop in the price of ETS permits to a point where they lost the power to incentivize emission reductions.

New Zealand's experience of introducing an emissions trading scheme to control greenhouse gas emissions has been unsuccessful too. Agriculture accounts for a large share of New Zealand's greenhouse gas emissions, but farmers have no access to a technology that enables them to reduce emissions within their prevailing farming systems. The agricultural sector has been held back from joining the emissions trading scheme pending the discovery of some viable technological solutions leaving the program as largely symbolic (Box 4.2).

Box 4.2 Failed Emission Trading in New Zealand

In 2009, the New Zealand government reaffirmed its intention to maintain an emissions trading scheme but with a number of concessions to ease the impact on business. These concessions recognized that New Zealand risked putting itself at an economic disadvantage if it moved too quickly.

- A price of $25 was fixed for Government-issued NZETS allowances (New Zealand Units, NZUs) used for compliance purposes during 2010–2012.
- Stationary energy, industrial process, and liquid fuel installations (the first sectors to join after forestry) need to surrender only 0.5 NZU for each tonne of carbon emitted.
- During the transition period (2010–2012), there is an unlimited supply of emissions allowances and so no overall cap on emissions.

- Emission-intensive industries exposed to international trade will receive the bulk of their allocation without cost. These are allocated on an intensity basis meaning that there is no penalty if total emissions increase providing that emissions per unit of output do not increase.
- The entry of sectors is sequenced according to the capacity to cut emissions without damaging their competitiveness in the international market place. This is to be judged overtime rather than according to a preset timetable.

The likelihood of the ETS being strengthened hinges partly on technology emerging that provides viable ways of reducing greenhouse gas emissions from agricultural activity. The Pastoral Greenhouse Gas Research Consortium (PGgRe) is supported by major rural industry agencies to coordinate industry-wide research into agricultural emissions and their reduction. Promising innovation to reduce emissions through the pasture application of nitrification inhibitors is claimed as well as the potential for soil carbon sequestration. On a larger scale, New Zealand in 2009 announced the formation of a Global Alliance on Agricultural Greenhouse Gas Mitigation to bring interested countries together to drive greater international cooperation, collaboration, and investment in this area of research.

In essence, emission trading relies on there being a good understanding of the costs of abatement and the availability of abatement options other than simply closing up business activity. More specifically, attention needs to be paid to at least four issues.

- There must be a relatively high level of knowledge about the environmental issue being managed and a degree of stability in the influences on the environmental outcomes. For example, if environmental risks were to change in an unanticipated way, the volume of permits allocated might give insufficient control. The difficulty of responding to any such instability arises because permits must be viewed as permanent and reliable if they are to influence business decisions. One response to this is to allow the total number of permits to vary depending on ecological or other conditions. This approach has been followed with fisheries management where tradable harvest quotas for fish are formulated as shares of a total allowable catch that is set according to the most recent fish population data. This flexibility is accepted as a broad principle as it is accepted that the dynamics of the ecosystem are difficult to predict much into the future. In practice, it can result in fisheries research becoming politicized as different parties seek to influence the form research takes, who undertakes and how data are interpreted.

- Trading systems need a sufficient number of parties to be involved to facilitate opportunities for the exchange of permits without encompassing enterprises operating in widely different sectors. It requires there to be a large variation in the costs of mitigating environmental impacts among the parties but also that there is in existence viable mitigation technology. Failing that, there needs to be a willingness among some economic parties to retire from the industry.

- The system for agreeing and registering trades of the permits needs to be simple as high transaction costs are a deterrent to trade. Recipients of permits must be willing to buy and sell permits if the environmental compliance effort is to be redistributed away from organizations facing the highest costs of making improvement. In industries with only a small number of participants, individual permit holders may be motivated to hoard them strategically as a way of making life hard for competitors.

- The use of tradable permits is difficult where localized pollution hot spots need to be controlled. Trading schemes have least risk where the environmental impacts are diffused over a wide area rather than being concentrated according to local conditions and the concentrations of emissions. This requirement is in tension with the previous point. The scheme must cover a large enough population to allow trading between polluters with varying costs of abatement if there are going to be cost savings in securing compliance to the total emission level. On the other hand, if the population occupies a geographical region comprising many different types of environment there is a likely to be a need to manage individual risks as well as the overall level of emissions. A possible response is to introduce administration controls to protect sensitive, most at risk localities but this type of intervention tends to substantially reduce the effectiveness of trading schemes.[10]

In brief, it seems that emission trading should be restricted to the management of a well understood environmental issue, where technological alternatives exist, the need for change is accepted and the program operates as a short-term adjustment scheme where the limited life of permits was signaled at the outset and the scheme is confined to a defined industry.

Environmental Offsets

As with the example of the CDM discussed above, "offsets" can be incorporated with a tradable permit scheme as well as being a management approach in their own right. The basic idea is to facilitate development that has undesired environmental costs by allowing it to be offset by other investment that has compensating outcomes. This offers a compromise to the proponents and opponents of new economic activity: a particular environment asset is allowed to be sacrificed on condition that this is compensated for by an equivalent improvement of some other environmental asset. When offsets work as intended, they can ensure that the total stock of environmental capital is not diminished even if some localized areas affected by development are degraded. Nonetheless, because there will always be uncertainty as to how closely the offset compensates for the damage resulting from new development offsetting is generally recognized to be an option of last resort. Offsetting should be allowed only if there is an overriding need for development that cannot proceed in any other form than that proposed.[11]

Offsets may be negotiated directly between a developer and an owner of a potential offset site or they might be managed by a private or public offset bank. An offset bank is a register of completed projects that have been assessed for their environmental values with these credits available for on-sale to a developer. The offset can include a trading ratio, whereby credits exceed estimated impacts. This can be presented as an opportunity to secure a net environmental gain although it can also be viewed as a margin for uncertainty and difference in the precise environmental qualities of the matched projects.

The acceptability of emission trading to manage greenhouse gas emissions to curb climate change has depended on the willingness of trading schemes to include provision for offsets.[12] To curb greenhouse gas emissions, the first option is that individuals and organizations lower their emissions directly by improving their energy efficiency, converting to lower emission alternatives, or changing their consumption patterns. These options exist for most business activities, although as noted above there are exceptions such as agriculture. In the case of greenhouse gases, the need to demonstrate offsetting is a "last resort" option has been weakened by the argument that the geographical location of a mitigation measure is irrelevant to its effect on global warming. This has encouraged the acceptance of offsetting to reduce the cost of meeting reduction targets as well as to accommodate those activities which have limited means to reduce their emissions short of ceasing activity entirely.[13]

A need for clear rules to ensure the legitimacy of offsets allowed into an emission trading scheme is heightened where there is geographical separation of the activity seeking an emission offset and the offset project. Offsetting as envisaged originally assumed a close connection between the environmental assets that are being offset: for example, if part of a wet land area was lost to development, an equivalent area of degraded wetland within the same ecosystem would be improved and protected. As the distance between connected projects increases so does the need for clear and precise accounting rules. Consequently, while *additionality* is a basic requirement whenever offsetting is allowed it has become of particular importance when judging the acceptability of offset projects allowed into greenhouse gas emission trading schemes.[14]

Additionality refers to the requirement that the reductions in emissions arising from the offset would not have otherwise occurred had the need for the offset not arisen. This is necessary to substantiate that someone or some organization somewhere has reduced an equivalent volume of emissions as those that are created by another development project going ahead. A prerequisite is that the offset project (which in practical terms may be something like planting a forest or replacing a coal-burning power station by a sustainable source of energy generation such as wind or solar) goes ahead only because of the need for the offset. The problem is that many of the projects being presented as offsets might have occurred under normal circumstances. For example, a windfarm may be presented as an offset on the grounds that it produces power with few greenhouse gas emissions and allows the retirement of alternative greenhouse gas generating forms of power. The difficulty is that the windfarm project may go ahead without it being identified as an offset, in which case it cannot truly claim to provide any additional benefit to the environment. Similarly, in the normal course of events, forest companies plant new areas of forest to supply their ongoing timber harvest needs and so by a strict additionality test new planting is not eligible to count as an offset. An exception might be if the forest were planted without intention of using it to support the commercial operations of the forest company.

As the range of potential offset projects increases so does the administrative demands in ensuring that only eligible projects are allowed as offsets and that the environmental credits claimed for the offset are accurate and certain of being achieved.[15] A range of either project-based or performance standard tests have been devised to check that each offset is judged appropriately, but in practice, there is often a tradeoff between the reliability of the test employed and the preference for administrative simplicity.[16]

Project-based tests offer a variety of ways of judging whether individual offset projects might have progressed without the need for the emissions saving but all tend ultimately to rely on a subjective assessment of the motivations for the offset. For example, an investment test assumes that an offset project is additional if it would have a lower than acceptable rate of return without revenue from the sale of its offset credits. Using this test ideally means knowing what the actual rate of return achieved is and what return would normally be required. Performance standards avoid the need for case-by-case evaluations by specifying thresholds for technologies or projects to determine additionality. In this approach, any use of a particular type of equipment or any project below a baseline level of emissions occurring in specified places might be taken to indicate sufficient deviation from the "business as usual" situation to be considered additional. Difficulties can be reduced by employing a mix of methods to judge additionality and by adding a margin to take account of the possibility that a proportion of the offsets may have occurred without any additional incentive. A further measure is to require offsets to demonstrate environmental benefits beyond the focal issue.

Experience with Environmental Offsets

Administrative integrity is essential to maintaining the effectiveness of offset projects to fulfill their role of compensating for the impacts of new development or the pollution generated by ongoing emissions. The administrative demands are high as program administrators must verify the reliability of the claimed debits and credits to know whether there is a genuine offset. For regulated parties, offsetting broadens the choice of reduction options and so generally makes regulation with the inclusion of an offset provision more attractive than one without. The danger is that provided the offset project is allowed by the regulator, the purchaser of the offset project has little reason to be concerned about the quality of the service that they purchase. The development of intermediary agencies that operate some form of offset trading register potentially introduces an element of quality control but they are potentially conflicted by their desire to encourage the use of offsets.

The Clean Development Mechanism (CDM) has been presented as a particularly high quality form of offset (sometimes referred to as a "gourmet offset") on account of its procedures for establishing additionality, project registration, and monitoring and its expectation that offset projects simultaneously have strong social and environmental benefits.[17] As the projects must be implemented in developing countries, the CDM is seen as a way of encouraging voluntary participation in efforts to reduce greenhouse gases in return for payments from developed countries who in turn benefit from the reduce cost of meeting emission reduction targets.[18] Nonetheless, doubts have grown as to whether the overall consequences of the CDM are positive for the environment.[19]

- The relative impact of a tonne of carbon emitted is the same whatever the source location, but this does not mean that offsetting is a perfect substitute for cutbacks directly in industrialized nations. Differing reductions may have varying long-term impacts depending on how they are achieved. A project based on facilitating a switch from private to public transport may have better chance of surviving long-term than an offset project based on substituting a sustainable source of energy for a carbon-based source of energy. Shifts in the relative costs of different energy sources may result in the offset project becoming uneconomic.
- Encouraging offsets can bring barriers to the future regulation of emission sources. Beneficiaries from the sale of *carbon credits* may oppose regulation that would deny them that revenue.
- The emissions that would have occurred if the market for offsets did not exist must be estimated in order to calculate the quantity of emissions reductions that the project achieves. Additionality testing is imperfect as the true counterfactual situation that would exist without the offset project cannot be known for sure.
- The CDM as with other offset markets are subject to "moral hazard." In "normal" markets the interests of the buyer and seller tend to work in opposite directions whereas in an offset market both the buyer and seller benefit from maximizing the number of offsets a project generates. This implies a need for tight regulation and ongoing monitoring but with this comes with administrative costs and delays. In 2010, it took an average 572 days for a CDM project to go through validation and registration and another 607 days until first issuance.[20]
- Maintaining the independence and neutrality of the auditors who verify emission reductions has proved a much greater

challenge than anticipated. Auditors must balance their business interest in maintaining relationships with project proponents against the reliability of their audits.

- A justification for the CDM was that it would involve projects that have potential for generating other environmental and social benefits for developing countries. In practice, the offset cobenefits to host countries from CDM projects have been limited especially in the extent of their impact on poor communities without access to energy services. In the context of forestry projects, it has been observed that they have typically been driven from the top down and not well integrated into the priorities of communities where they occur.[21] Projects based on capturing methane from landfills have been accused of extending the life of a landfill that otherwise would be closed because of its proximity to human settlement.[22]

A broader question raised by the use of emission trading and offsetting is its impact in encouraging innovation to help industry ultimately operate with reduced environmental impact. A danger with any form of regulation is that it shifts the focus of business from pursuing innovation of long-term significance to a focus on pursuing forms of innovation that help it deal with the immediate demands of the regulation. An underlying justification for the switch to market-based regulation is that it maximizes the incentive to go beyond the minimum requirements of regulation. The suggestion has been made that emission trading maximizes short-term positioning without increasing the incentive to pursue long-term technological advancement.[23] Further research is needed to confirm this, but meanwhile, it is certainly evident that much of the innovation arising from the emission trading of greenhouse gases has partly taken the form of a "race-to-the-bottom" in search of the lowest cost offset projects.[24]

Chapter Summary

Emission trading has gained attention as a way of regulating the emissions of greenhouse gases. With emission trading entities are allocated permits which are in effect permits to pollute. The theory is that some companies will not need all their permits, perhaps because of their up-to-date production methods that emit comparatively small amounts of pollution. By allowing surplus permits to be sold, good performers are rewarded while poor performers are penalized by needing to buy additional permits. The acid rain program is presented as a model for the effectiveness of emission trading, but it has proved to be hard to replicate this success when applying it to the control of greenhouse gas emissions. Offsets can be part of emission trading. They enable credits to be earned by investing in projects that produce benefits that can used to cancel (offset) emissions for which permits would otherwise need to be held. This can help new development to proceed without causing any new environmental loss, but it does require additional administration to ensure the offset gains are real. The use of offsets for gaining carbon credits has highlighted many areas of poor practice.

Key Concepts

Additionality: change that occurs as a result of regulation that is in addition to that which would have occurred in the absence of the regulation.

Bubbles: an aspect of an emission trading program where the emissions of multiple individual sources are treated as a single emission for the purpose of measuring the level of emissions.

Cap and trade: a feature of emission trading where a cap (limit) is based on the maximum volume of emissions for which permits will be allowed; the cap may be lowered over time where the program objective is to eradicate or at least significantly reduce emissions.

Carbon credits: credits earned by investing in schemes which reduce total carbon emissions, also can be called carbon offsets.

Clean development mechanism (CDM): a feature of the Kyoto Protocol to the UN Framework Convention on Climate Change that provides an opportunity for companies to earn carbon credits by investing on carbon mitigation projects in developing economies. CDM projects are reviewed and endorsed by a UN agency. Following the expiry of the Kyoto Protocol in 2012, the future of the CDM was uncertain.

Emission trading: buying and selling the right to emit a pollutant based on the allocation of emission permits.

Environmental charges: a tax or other financial payment levied on an activity for the purposes of seeking to discourage the activity because of the environmental damage it causes, also known as green taxes or eco taxes. The revenue raised may be used to address the environmental damage related or become part of a government's general budget revenue. Taxes can usually only be imposed by national governments so payments are usually referred to as charges when levied by other public agencies such as local government.

European Union ETS: The European Union emission trading scheme introduced to control greenhouse gas emissions.

Grandfathering: a system for allocating emission permits or ITQ in which the initial distribution is made according to the proportion of emissions (or for ITQs, the proportion of the resource used or collection) that the company accounted for prior to the start of emission trading.

Greenhouse gas: any gas that absorbs infrared radiation in the atmosphere, contributing to the warming of the earth's temperature; this includes carbon dioxide, methane, nitrous oxide, and chloroflurocarbons.

Individual transferable quota (ITQ): an entitlement to a share of a resource that can be bought and sold; can be used to allocate a right to harvest a specified volume of a specified fish species.

Kyoto Protocol: An international agreement initially adopted on 11 December 1997 in Kyoto, Japan and that was in force from 2005 to 2012 as a protocol governing climate change policies of countries that signed the agreement. It was the first major achievement of the UN Framework Convention on Climate Change.

Offset: credit (positive environmental gain) obtained from a project undertaken to compensate for the negative environmental impact of another project (which may be a wholly new project or existing activity that comes within the sphere of regulation).

Pigovian tax: a tax imposed on an activity that is set to match the value of the environmental damage caused by the activity. The willingness to pay the tax indicates that tax payers prefer the loss of environment to a curtailment of the activity that causes environmental damage.

Tradable permits: a right to a specified amount of environmental impact, such as a volume of greenhouse gas emissions, that can be used or traded and which usually form part of an emissions trading scheme, also known as transferable permits.

Endnotes

1. Driesen (2010).
2. Sterner (2003), p. 82.
3. De Freitas and Perry (2012).
4. Parry (2002).
5. Congressional Budget Office (2000).
6. Goulder (2000).
7. See Corbera and Brown (2010).
8. Driesen (2010) drawing on Kete (1992); van Dyke (1999).
9. See Schmalensee and Stavins (2012); Sterner and Coria (2012).
10. Sterner (2003), p. 88.
11. Pearce and Warford (1993); Landry *et al.* (2005).
12. Kollmuss *et al.* (2008).
13. Corbera and Brown (2009).
14. Kollmuss *et al.* (2008).
15. Driesen(1998); (2010).
16. Kollmuss *et al.* (2008).
17. As well as the CDM, the Kyoto Protocol allowed Joint Implementation as another form of offset.
18. Boyd (2009).
19. See Kollmuss *et al.* (2008), pp. 89–90; Driesen (2010).
20. Kossoy and Ambrosi (2010), p. 47.
21. Boyd (2009).
22. Driesen (2010), p. 8.
23. Driesen (2010).
24. Kysar and Meyler (2008).

CHAPTER 5

Administering Regulation

The discussion so far has emphasized how any form of regulation, including command and control has its own strengths and weaknesses. There is no single way of implementing regulation that is obviously superior to all others or that should be regarded as the default first option to employ. Rather than leading to the recommendation of one approach that is inherently efficient and effective, awareness of the diversity of regulatory styles and what each has to offer is important. Smart regulation is about the overall approach to administering regulation more than the judicious selection of the "one best way" to design intervention. This chapter substantiates this claim in two ways. First, it elaborates the distinction introduced in Chapter 1 between normative and political economy interpretations of policy selection. This distinction draws attention to the institutional pressures that can encourage convergence on a particular regulatory style. Second, it discusses five administrative principles that have been proposed as the basis for making smart regulation. These principles form part of the original guide to smart environmental regulation to which this book adds a sixth principle.[1] This chapter reviews and updates the five principles in the light of experience and the discussion of information sharing and emissions trading in Chapters 3 and 4.

Making Policy Choices

The recent debate about environmental regulation has been strongly influenced by arguments that one approach is largely ineffective (command and control) while another (market-based regulation) is efficient and effective. This context makes it relevant to ask how policy choices are made. Broadly, two interpretations exist, which summarized simply identify how policy decisions ought to be made (*normative guidance*) versus how they are made in practice (*political economy*).[2]

Normative Guidance

Economic analysis can recommend when a particular tool is likely to be more or less appropriate, but it does not offer a simple set of instructions. A wide range of influences need to be considered when determining which particular policy approach is likely to be most effective. One set of considerations relate to the costs organizations may face to improve their performance.

- If the costs to individual organizations to achieve a comparable level of performance vary widely, it implies that some organizations have potentially large expenditures to make relative to other organizations. These circumstances suggest a management tool that equalizes the expenditure made by organizations rather than the performance level attained.
- Where there is confidence in the ability of technological change to reduce environmental improvement costs, there is opportunity to envisage a comparatively rapid escalation in the performance level targeted by regulation. This suggests a management approach that can rapidly adjust the target aimed for.

A second set of considerations relate to the nature of the environmental damages that are to be managed.

- Where the incidence of environmental damage from activity or emissions is affected by the precise location, time, or other circumstances surrounding the emission, it is generally necessary to exercise control of all individual emission sources. This tends to rule out forms of regulation that give flexibility to industries and organizations over the allocation of abatement effort.

- Some environmental issues such as those associated with the use of industrial chemicals and agricultural pesticides are complex in the sense that the precise usage and mixing of substances affects the level of environmental risk. Environmental impacts arising from a combination of circumstances generally need to be managed by responses customized to their particular circumstances.
- If environmental impacts are sensitive to a particular threshold value, a high level of assurance that impacts stay below that level is needed. This implies that regulation will need to provide a high degree of assurance that the threshold will not be breached.

A third set of issues relate to the practical ability to control an environment issue.

- The effectiveness of an intervention is influenced by the ability to observe that people and organizations are complying with the regulation or at least that regulated entities perceive that they are potentially under surveillance. In the case of environmental impacts that arise from numerous, small-scale, intermittent, and dispersed actions, the ease of evasion is a challenge to using forms of regulation that rely on monitoring and enforcement action.
- Where an industry generating an environmental problem is dominated by a small number of businesses, the possibility for strategic responses agreed among industry participants is greater than where industry ownership is fragmented among many independent enterprises. Regulation may need to consider the scope for strategic action to frustrate environmental policy objectives.

Assessing such considerations provides general guidance on what conditions suit what type of management approach (Table 5.1). This type of guidance can be refined further to the selection of individual instruments (emissions trading, environmental taxes, standards and so on).[3]

Table 5.1 Normative guidance for regulation design[4]

Regulation design	Conditions supporting the regulation
Emission trading	Environmental damage depends on the overall amount of a pollutant and not on the specific location of individual emission sources or the timing of emissions relative to other emissions.
	Technological options exist that are within the reach of most industry participants or acceptable offset options exist in lieu of the ability to make reductions at source.
	The industry population encompasses a sufficient number of enterprises that vary in their preference to reduce emissions versus paying for emissions.
	Sufficient institutional capacity and experience exists to set the volume of emissions.
	There is a low risk of external shocks such as changes in market conditions or changes in technology affecting the value of emissions permits.
Environmental taxes	Pollution sources are small and diffuse so that environmental damage depends more on the overall level of pollution rather than on the geographical distribution of pollution sources, local environmental conditions, or the timing of pollution emissions.
	Payment for environmental damage is an acceptable alternative for avoiding the damage.
Subsidy of preferred technology or compensation for retired production	Activity to be subsidized is a strong substitute for the targeted "dirty" activity that the regulations seek to reduce or close down.
	Subsidy program does not encourage over investment in the subsidized activity, implying change can be affected over short time period with a subsidy having few secondary effects.
Deposit-refund systems	Deposit does not provide an incentive for corruption (i.e., bogus product created merely to collect the deposit).
	Modest deposit value sufficient to modify behavior.
	Environmental issue is contained by the collection of material; there is no scope or need to eradicate the use of the product on which a deposit is paid.
Performance-based command and control	Performance-based requirements can be expressed in a clear and precise manner to ensure sufficient action to control the environmental issue is taken.
	The best available method for attaining the environmental objectives varies according to the size, location, workforce, technology, or other characteristics of firms.
	Eradication of environmental damage at source is not feasible; it is necessary to manage impact by management processes that minimize hazards and contain pollution.

Regulation design	Conditions supporting the regulation
Technology standard-based command and control	Little variation in pollution control costs between polluters. Technology utilized is similar across producers irrespective of firm characteristics.
Support for development of environmental technology and "green" innovation	New technology requires large market take-up and experience gained through use, creating barriers to its diffusion without public sector support. Technology uptake depends on development of supporting infrastructure prior to which there is a need for public support the use of the technology. Uncertainty exists over the most viable technologies on which to base innovation.
Industry self-regulation	Industry associations are able to exercise authority by withholding the association's endorsement from firms not complying with the industry's regulation. Absence of mandatory regulation provides a strong incentive for industry to put their own regulation in place. Self-regulation does not compromise the option of introducing mandatory regulation should this be required.

Normative recommendations provide a starting point for discussion as policy makers may have other concerns to attend to beyond the containment of an environmental issue. For example, environmental management objectives may need to be modified according to expected levels of inflation since high inflation will undermine the impact of a fixed charge or monetary incentive. The relative burden on high- and low-income households may need to modify ideal choices or at least require that the impacts of regulation can be offset through some form of income redistribution. Finally, if the burden of regulation falls disproportionally on one sector or has particular consequences for some businesses more than others, the ability to overcome resistance to the policy will need to be considered. It is also important to recognize that the normative guidance leaves detailed aspects of any regulatory design to be resolved. The selection of emissions trading, for example, needs to be followed with decisions about the allocation of permits, the volume of emissions permitted, the speed and scale of reductions in the cap, bubble and offsetting provisions and so on. Nonetheless, the existence of normative guidance is important as it indicates the need to fit regulation to the characteristics of the environmental issue of concern.

Political Economy Guidance

Normative guidance exists, but it is unclear that it played a major role in encouraging the shift from command and control to market-based regulation. It is possible to explain this change by reference to the social forces that encouraged a collective belief that sustainability was best addressed through market-based approaches. In other words, to draw on a concept introduced in Chapter 2, "institutional isomorphism" rather than evidence of effectiveness turned decision makers away from "command and control" approaches.

Prior to the widespread concern with sustainability, the use of command and control approaches was broadly accepted although alternative approaches were known about from economic theory. Interested parties had different reasons for their support of command and control.[5]

- For industry lobby groups, the tendency for regulation to adopt an industry-by-industry focus made command and control a comparatively acceptable approach. Industry representation tends to be fragmented among industry-based associations reflecting how business support of collective action is easier to coordinate when it deals with issues of concern to small groups.[6] Business lobby groups perceived their task was easier if regulation targeted a single industry than if regulation addressed multiple industries and had a focus on the quantity of pollution, not who generates it or the technology used.

- Environmental campaign groups opposed market-based instruments as they were likened to a "license to pollute" and had the implication that environmental damage can be accommodated provided it is paid for. Environmentalists favored giving control of the use of the environment to public agencies whereas market-based instruments implied the devolution of control to the businesses being regulated.

- Labor groups supported command and control regulation as it was seen as less threatening to the protection of jobs in heavy polluting activities. A shift to market-based instruments implied a relocation of activity to newer, cleaner businesses.

- Policy makers had most familiarity with command and
  control regulation and resisted innovation with policy that
  had uncertain outcomes, were potentially highly contentious,
  and that potentially implied a scaled-down role for
  government agencies.

The consensus in favor of command and control regulation broke down during the 1990s. This was part of a shift in political outlook in favor of deregulation and the greater use of market forces to address social and economic problems, as well as changes in perception specific to the environmental policy agenda. This was a time when society-wide agreement grew over critical environmental issues, including damage to the ozone layer through CFC emissions, the impact of acid rain, and the environmental damage of lead in petrol. With more aspects of environmental performance under the spotlight and higher expectations of the targets to be pursued, the costs of pollution control became a concern. For example, in the United States, the costs of pollution control to industry were estimated as growing nearly 300 percent during 1972–1990.[7] This encouraged interest in market-based approaches as a more cost-effective way of affecting change than the use of traditional regulation.

Environmental groups too became receptive to market-based approaches particularly after it appeared that tradable permit programs had contributed to three issues of wide concern: sulfur dioxide, lead in gasoline, and CFC emissions. In each of these cases, absolute reduction in emissions had been achieved not simply a reallocation of responsibility based on the cost of control. With no prior policy interest in many environmental issues addressed through market-based approaches, there was no lobby aligned to an existing, alternative policy regime that had to be overcome.

Implications of Alternative Policy Selection Processes

From the perspective of designing smart regulation, it is not necessary to determine which of these approaches provides the better account of how policy selections have really been made. In reality, some mix of influences is likely to exist. More importantly than determining which offers most insight, both lead to the same overall conclusion: good regulatory design comes from customizing intervention to the circumstances of the problem addressed, more by learning through experience than following a prescribed form of best practice regulation. Normative guidance is not sufficiently developed to provide a policy rulebook. It offers some broad starting points for policy design that require customization to the particular context and objectives of regulation. Recognizing that institutional pressure can influence policy choices should give reason to consider design options beyond the currently fashionable and politically preferred approaches.

Principles of Smart Regulation

Five principles of good practice in administering regulation have been proposed.[8] This section summarizes these principles, reviews their usefulness, and where appropriate revises the original principle in the light of policy experience over the last decade. For comparison, the original versions of the principles are given in Table 5.2, which also shows the addition of one new principle.

Table 5.2 Original and reformulated principles of smart environmental regulation

Gunningham, Grabosky, and Sinclair principle (1998)	Revised/new principle
Prefer policy mixes incorporating a broader range of instruments and institutions	Utilize a mix of regulatory styles rather than a single form of regulation
Prefer less interventionist measures	Minimize the extent of intervention
Ascend a dynamic instrument pyramid to the extent necessary to achieve policy goals	Build responsiveness into policy programs
Empower participants which are in the best position to act as surrogate regulators	Maximize the use of nongovernmental regulators
Maximize opportunities for win–win outcomes	Win–win outcomes are encouraged through regulation
	Smart regulation is built through smart policy evaluation

Principle 1: Utilize a Mix of Regulatory Styles
Rather than a Single form of Regulation

There is no absolute rule that it is always best to use a mix of regulatory approaches to address an issue, but generally, it is most effective and
efficient to do so. For example, the desire to stop the use of a dangerous chemical outright suggests the relevance of a command and control
approach. Assuming the chemical is dangerous in whatever the context
in which it is used, the need is to ensure absolute conformance to the
same behavior. Even so, the time and effort taken to obtain compliance
is likely to be minimized where an element of responsiveness and risk-
based enforcement is utilized as well. In addition, drawing in appropriate gatekeepers to help educate chemical users and spread monitoring
capacity is potentially justified too. These additional approaches will be
particularly useful where production and use of the chemical is comparatively invisible.

A principle of smart regulation is that combinations of regulatory design tend to be more effective than pursuing one approach at the expense
of another. A contradiction potentially exists between encouraging a di-
versification of regulation styles and the benefit of consistency in the ways
that business managers experience regulation. Where government admin-
istrations use a variety of regulatory designs, this may mean divergent
approaches are taken according to the issues to which regulation are addressed. As pointed out by the proponents of smart regulation, avoiding
differences in the way regulators interact with regulated parties is at least
as important as assuring that each area of regulation is fit for purpose.
Having a diversity of regulatory styles risks regulated parties forming
judgments of regulators based on their least preferred form of regulation. This may mean, for example, a responsive style of regulation may be
undermined by regulated parties also having experience of a command-
and-control style of regulation that gives little or no scope to follow an
enforcement strategy based primarily on education and persuasion.

The recommendation to use a mix of styles is thus qualified by the
need for careful selection of the design combinations that are adopted,
including in the options the use of *hybrid regulation* where a single form
of intervention draws from two or more intervention styles.

"Smart" regulation aims to integrate policy interventions as well as select the most appropriate tool for any particular issue.[9] A broad claim, for example, is that requirements for better information will assist any other form of regulation.[10] For example, a lack of insight into how other businesses are responding to demands for improved environmental performance may hold back other companies from taking action, fearing they may find themselves at a competitive disadvantage. This is a major impediment to self-regulation but also affects the use of principle-based regulation, which will work only when there is confidence that a shared understanding exists of how principles should be responded to. As we have seen as well, responsive styles of regulation assume a degree of transparency in the operation of regulation and require individual companies to have some insight into how other companies are responding to the regulation. All of which implies that information disclosure may be viewed as something to be used in combination with other forms of regulation rather than as a standalone initiative.

The idea of mixing complementary regulatory approaches is most developed in the design of hybrid regulation, such as the proposal for mixing risk and responsive styles of regulation into an integrated approach for the management of environmental low risks.[11] Where the nature of the risk is low, a regulator is generally unable to justify the investment of significant agency resources to evaluate and manage risks, but some form of surveillance and enforcement is nonetheless required. Individually, sites or activities may be of low risk but still give rise to a considerable damage if impacts accumulate and in the process change the nature of the issue. As a general response to this context, Black and Baldwin devised the *Good Regulatory Intervention Design* (GRID) guide to the selection of enforcement approaches according to the nature of the low risk and the nature of the regulated party (Table 5.3).

The GRID framework recommends that three considerations inform the regulatory strategy adopted for low-risk activities:

- The characteristics of the regulated party: following standard responsiveness theory, the GRID recognizes that entities may be able and willing to comply while others are neither motivated nor well positioned to comply. Between these are those with varying degrees of motivation and ability to comply.

Table 5.3 Regulatory intensity proposed by GRID framework[12]

Nature of the regulated party	Nature of the low risk			
	Stable, inherent low risk	Stable, net low risk	Unstable, inherent low risk	Unstable, net low risk
Well motivated with high capacity to comply	Low	Low	Low	Low
Well motivated with low capacity to comply	Low	Low	Medium–low	Medium–low
Low motivation but with high capacity to comply	Medium	Medium	Medium	High
Low motivation and with low capacity to comply	Medium	Medium	High	High

- The nature of the risk: a source of risk may be inherently of low risk or only so because of management intervention. The level of risk may be unaffected by circumstance or change in potential severity according to the precise occurrence of risk events. These considerations differentiate low risks in the GRID and are used to recommend where surveillance and enforcement effort should be concentrated.
- Match enforcement to response: reflecting the low risk context (which may not justify ultimate command and control sanctions such as imprisonment), the GRID distinguishes screening tools (such as requiring registration, with or without conditions); inspection and monitoring tools (varying according to frequency, coverage, and postinspection action); and engagement and incentive strategies (including information sharing, dialog, and demonstration of solutions). As well as the choice of tools, regulatory intensity can vary in terms of the amount of time and effort allocated to one type of risk and regulated entity relative to another.

The GRID is recommended with two conditions. First, optimizing the GRID depends on learning from experience. To facilitate this, a *Good Regulatory Assessment Framework* (GRAF) is part of the GRID methodology to provide guidance on how to evaluate how well the initial regulatory approach is working. Second, the GRID should be customized to the particular expectations, costs and challenges of the issue being addressed, including the ability of regulators to make the astute assessments needed to classify risks and regulated entities. The impact of these conditions is illustrated by the way the GRID was modified when applied to one of the issues for which it was first developed: the regulation of domestic waste water treatment systems in Ireland (Box 5.1).

As emphasized by the designers of the GRID, there is no substitute for the insight gathered through experience, because, usually, there is a need to adapt regulation to the context in which it is applied. Regulators must expect to exercise judgment in risk targeting, selecting appropriate varieties of intervention options, and in optimizing the level of investigation within the available resources.[13] In the waste water example, primarily reliance on "bottom of the pyramid" enforcement measures is possible because environmental impacts fall on the property owner on whose land the systems are located rather than being exclusively externalities. There is likely to be less choice over the use of enforcement mechanisms where polluters have little self-interest in complying.

Box 5.1 Using the GRID for Regulating Domestic Wastewater Systems in Ireland

Domestic waste water systems mainly take the form of septic tanks that comprise a collection tank to hold waste water for bacterial processing prior to its drainage into an underground percolation area. Designed, installed, and operated appropriately, they pose low risks of pollution. Where systems malfunction over a long period of time, the environmental impact can nonetheless be significant, especially if the environment is sensitive or especially valued and if poorly performing systems are colocated. The initial GRID for this issue recognized only one type of risk: net low, dynamic risks (low risk depends on management and circumstances). Given the "out-of-sight, out-of-mind" nature of domestic water systems, it was judged that most septic tank owners had low motivation and low capacity to comply. This reduced the GRID to essentially determining the regulatory intensity (relative to other low risk sources), the choice of tools, and the sequence in which they would be deployed.

Following legislation requiring registration, an inspection plan and powers to seek remediation of faulty systems the GRID was amended to recognize two types of regulated entity: those that registered their systems and those did not. Drawing on inspector's reflections on what had been working, a combination of inspection and citizen engagement strategies were devised to motivate homeowners to maintain their systems adequately and make them knowledgeable to do so. This approach was put in place in 2013 and will require further time to prove its ultimate effectiveness. There is a comparative lack of understanding of which tools and strategies are most effective in containing which type of risk, and so, further need to modify the GRID should be expected.

Principle 2: Minimize the Extent of Intervention

Intervention in the context of regulation refers to the level of *prescription* and *coercion*. A highly prescriptive form of intervention gives little or no option as to the action to be taken. A coercive form of regulation has powers of enforcement to compel compliance among entities covered by the regulation. This principle has traditionally been interpreted as implying "avoid command and control," but this form of regulation does not have to imply a high level of prescription. As noted in the discussion of command and control, the prescribed performance may be broad as in seeking the adoption of "best practice."

Rather than interpreting this principle as minimizing the use of command and control approaches, it can be expressed in terms of the reasons why low intervention is a preferred approach. Low intervention is advantageous where:

- There are a variety of ways that businesses and other entities can meet the objectives of the regulation, such as investing in the most modern equipment or modifying older technology.
- A prescriptive and coercive approach has potential to provoke opposition to the regulation, increasing the effort required to obtain compliance compared with a more flexible form of regulation.
- There is a net saving in monitoring and enforcement costs, which might, for example, be achieved by the lack of intervention being reciprocated by a willingness among some parties to go beyond what highly prescriptive regulation required.
- There is more support for a low intervention approach so that resources otherwise devoted to overcoming opposition can be saved.
- A low-intervention approach does not compromise the possibility of subsequently shifting to a more interventionist approach if this proves necessary. Such a shift might be comprised where a delay in securing a change in behavior modifies the nature of the environment risk.

These considerations may be assessed differently by small and large business. A response may be to target a more interventionist program on those most willing to accept this form of regulation. When expressed in terms of firm attributes such as size or financial resources, this may create problems setting and enforcing a boundary. The use of some form of metaregulation may be a more acceptable approach in which demonstration of certain management practices (perhaps confirmed through certification) is required to be exempt from the more interventionist form of a policy program.

Principle 3: Build Responsiveness into Policy Programs

The third principle is the general desirability of building a degree of responsiveness into the administration of regulation. This recommendation is consistent with the comment in Chapter 2 that responsiveness is better viewed as a way of implementing regulation rather than a separate style of its own right. The regulator's interaction with regulated parties is most considered but there is an argument that *really responsive* regulation is responsive on several further dimensions too (Box 5.2).

Box 5.2 Dimensions of Really Responsive Regulation[14]

The success of regulation depends on regulation-setting agencies being attentive of their response to the following considerations.

The attitudes and outlooks of regulated parties: a mix of rational (evidence-informed) and institutional pressure (shaped by industry culture, market dynamics, and related influences) shape how regulated parties respond to regulation and the agenda set by a regulatory agency. To be effective, public agencies need to understand the context in which they are introducing regulation and how this may affect its reception.

Institutional environments: the organizational context of the agency responsible for regulation in terms of the resources, decision-making authority, role clarity, and overall status in the government system affects the operation of regulation.

Regulation selection and implementation: agencies need to administer regulation according to the needs of the regulation, the objectives set and the perceptions of regulated parties. This sensitivity requires flexibility in agency behavior, good communication, and the management of overlapping jurisdictions involved in the implementation of regulation.

Performance monitoring: agencies need to adjust regulation and agency strategies in the light of insight into program performance.

Environmental change: developments in markets, technology, political and public expectations, and institutional structures can affect the operation of regulation.

Application of this principle partly depends on the existence of a spectrum of enforcement mechanisms commencing with self-regulation and ending with legal enforcement and significant penalties for noncompliance. The principle as originally proposed also assumes the viability of information sharing as a viable starting point for regulation. The discussion in Chapters 1 and 3 has raised questions about the reliability of self-regulation and information sharing as alternatives to more prescriptive forms of regulation. Two techniques enabling a degree of enforcement sequencing have been proposed that offer some potential to build responsiveness into regulation: *triggers* and *circuit breakers*.

A trigger refers to setting some form of threshold beyond which it is deemed enforceable regulation is needed to control the activity in question. The use of a trigger to signal a point where regulation commences can give space for self-regulation as a starting point for control. Two considerations shape the potential impact of defining a trigger point. First, the assumption is that business will prefer the option of a voluntary response over the need to comply with a mandated program. In practice, the strength of this preference is likely to vary according to the number of industry participants and perceived risk of "free riding." Business are more likely to agree significant self-regulation in a context where it is comparatively easy to observe noncompliance and where there is scope to use informal pressure to bring under performers up to the required performance level. As discussed in Chapter 2, the difficulty of agreeing voluntary action among large numbers of enterprises aligned with doubts over the reliability of surveillance by regulatory bodies are barriers to seeking change through self-regulation even this is linked to a threat of formal regulation.

Second, a time lag between signaling the intention to commence enforcement and its impact on business behavior may make it necessary to trigger regulation early when impacts are still at a low level. This is to control the risk of environment damage arising before enforcement action starts to bite. Practically, this means, therefore, that there may be a small margin of tolerance before enforcement action of some form is needed.

Circuit breakers offer scope for building in a form of responsiveness by removing a barrier to the use of a preferred regulatory response. As a measure that is utilized for the purpose of enabling some other form of intervention to occur, the circuit breaker is expected to be a short-term measure. Circuit breakers can take the form of some form of financial inducement or they may involve the temporary exclusion of some sectors or types of enterprise from the coverage of the policy instrument that ultimately is expected to encompass all parts of the economy. The justification for such concessions is that some form of compromise will overcome resistance that otherwise risks absorbing considerable regulatory effort to secure the desired change, including a potentially unacceptable level of enforcement effort to secure compliance. The use of deposit-refund schemes and offsetting are two specific ways of delivering a circuit breaker, which illustrate some of the potential and shortcomings of their use.

Deposit-Refund as a Circuit Breaker.   Deposit-refund schemes provide an incentive to comply with an environmental goal (such as waste and pollution control) by combining a charge (paid as a refundable deposit) and a subsidy (the refund payment given on return). They can be used as a circuit breaker where there is a desire to change individual behavior and: (i) regulation would stand to be devalued by the difficulty of monitoring compliance; (ii) where the environmental damage is associated with the way a product is disposed of after its use; (iii) where the goal is to eradicate the damage, not merely require payment as a compensation for damage. The deposit-refund approach makes polluters pay a charge only if they do not collect back their deposit. This mechanism gives deposit-refund schemes a high degree of self-management to the extent that the incentive to obtain a refund of the deposit encourages the behavioral change sought by the regulation. This use of a circuit breaker is well established in the case of beverage containers and less frequently with other small items such as car batteries. Where schemes operate, recovery rates for drink containers can be as high as 98% for glass bottles. Interestingly, the recovery rate does not seem to be sensitive to the size of the refund.[15]

The possibility of using deposit-refund schemes as a temporary measure to institute waste minimizing behavior is suggested by the high rates of product return possible with purely voluntary recycling schemes for glass, plastics, and paper. This suggests the importance of information, opinion, values, and habits in encouraging the participation in recycling rather than the need for an ongoing financial incentive. Of particular importance is the ease of being able to fit recycling into everyday activity without the need for special journeys or adherence to specific collection schedules. Even long distance travel need not be a barrier, provided that it can be integrated with other routine activity.

The extension of deposit-refund schemes to more valuable or pollution intensive items is limited by the risk of abusing the availability of refund payments. Rogue imports from other countries for the sole purpose of collecting refunds need to be screened out. Sweden did operate a deposit-refund scheme for motor vehicles to control the dumping of scrapped vehicles. The deposit was successful in getting a car's last owners to return their cars, but it did not provide an incentive for modifying motor vehicles to increase the scope for recycling and product improvement.[16] For these reasons, the scheme was replaced by a more ambitious product stewardship scheme in 1997 that required manufacturers and importers of cars registered after the scheme's introduction to accept end-of-life vehicles free-of-charge. Built into the scheme are targets for the proportion of materials in vehicles that can be reused or recycled. The stewardship approach is more onerous than traditional deposit-refund schemes, but it has two in-built circuit breakers: product distributors can charge buyers with the costs of the stewardship responsibilities; management of the returned product is determined through goal setting plans rather than mandated targets.

Offsetting as a Circuit Breaker.   Offsetting is another form of circuit breaker, which, as discussed in Chapter 4 has been used to gain agreement for the introduction of emission trading schemes. Given the well-established nature of offsetting as an aspect of emission trading, it might be questioned whether this is consistent with the use of circuit breakers as short-lived measures. One reason for suggesting this is the review of offsetting provisions that is taking place as a component of any post-Kyoto protocol agreement following widespread doubts that offsetting as worked as intended. This experience (as summarized in Chapter 4) indicates the importance of designing circuit breakers that do make compliance too easy or that provide an incentive for third parties to aid the use of the circuit breaker to the detriment of the larger policy objectives.

Offsetting has a potential role to play when there is little or no scope to avoid environmental damage and a strong case for development exists. Some basic rules of offsetting do need to be maintained to ensure development at least ensures no net environmental damage occurs.

- They are a last resort measure to be used only in cases where environmental impacts cannot be reduced at source and when forgoing the development is not an acceptable alternative.
- The offset includes a trading ratio whereby credits exceed estimated impacts to accommodate a margin for uncertainty and difference in the precise environmental qualities of the matched projects.
- A strong additionality test is applied to ensure that the offset project occurs only because of the need to offset the development project.
- Even with the inclusion of a trading margin, there is a precise match between the environmental impacts of the development and the environmental gains of the offset project. This includes minimizing the geographical separation.
- Offset projects that are negotiated on a case-by-case basis are preferable to the option of allowing the accumulation of offset projects in some form of offset bank: banking risks making it comparatively easy to access offset opportunities whereas they should be viewed as a last resort option used only if emissions cannot be reduced at source.

Principle 4: Maximize the Use of Nongovernmental Regulators

This principle was reflected in the discussion of principle-based regulation (Chapter 2), which identified networked PBR as a distinct form of this approach to regulation. It features as a particular concern of principle-based regulation because the obligations imposed by this form of regulation can be open to wide interpretation. This potentially places a heavy burden on regulators if they alone are required to provide guidance on compliance. For regulated parties, networked PBR can reduce the effort to design compliance strategies and increase their confidence in the steps taken by ensuring their consistency with how similar entities are advised to act too.

The more general case for involving nongovernmental regulators is that they can exercise more leverage over-regulated parties than a government agency. Beyond the general possibility that facilitating nongovernment participation in the administration of regulation will diffuse the tendency for regulation to be viewed as "us versus them" phenomenon, increasing its acceptability, nongovernment parties can variously offer four sources of leverage over regulated parties.

- A third party may control resources critical to the operation of a business, giving it a direct and powerful means of sanctioning a company. Banks and insurance companies have been identified as potential *quasi regulators* on this basis.
- Another commercial entity or collective industry body may be perceived as understanding commercial realities and have more credibility with private business than government regulators.
- To the extent that under resourcing is typical of government agencies, and under resourcing affects the authority of agencies and their ability to act, drawing in other parties can supplement regulatory effort.
- Particularly where the number of regulated parties is large and their location dispersed, it may be practically impossible for a government agency to identify, educate, and monitor them. Nongovernment agencies may have better reach or at least provide an extension to the reach of official regulators.

As well as involving nongovernmental regulators in a principle-based approach, they may be involved as a first response within a responsive pyramid of enforcement that ultimately sees a transfer of responsibility to government regulators. Of course, inviting multiple parties to participate in the regulatory process can risk generating conflicting advice and exposing regulated parties to poorly informed guidance. Consequently, the principle has been rewritten from that proposed originally, which was "empower participants which are in the best position to act as surrogate regulators."[17] The best position alone may not justify drawing a third party into the regulation process. Some form of qualification process can help to reduce these risks by giving delegation to selected third parties based on their willingness and capacity to act. Even then, realizing the theoretical potential of nongovernment regulators is not straightforward as potential candidates for the role are frequently not in a strong position to take on the task.

Industry and trade associations are the form of collective body most joined by individual businesses: most businesses have at least one such association to join and most associations succeed in attracting most of the members they aspire to represent.[18] These qualifications are also associated with the inherent weakness of most industry associations to act as regulators: high rates of membership are required for business associations to act as representatives and lobbyists for their constituency. Minimizing the obligations on members is a primary means of recruitment when high rates of membership are the priority and the major benefits of association activity are obtained by members and nonmembers alike.[19] This typically explains why business associations do not enforce compliance with codes of practice as a membership requirement and indicates that they are not well placed to employ other tools of regulatory enforcement. Moreover, trade associations are not necessarily well resourced to take on the role of regulator, and it cannot be assumed that they seek involvement in enforcing regulation (Box 5.3).

Box 5.3 New Zealand Chemical Industry Council (NZCIC) on Principle-Based Regulation[20]

The NZCIC is an industry association with a membership of around 145 mainly small organizations but also including the local operations of multinational companies. This association assists member firms comply with hazardous substances control legislation. This legislation mainly takes the form of performance-based outcomes that specify what organizations are expected to achieve, without indicating how they are to be achieved.

A 24-hour emergency response system and codes of practice indicating how to comply with regulatory requirements are among the ways NZCIC helps members meet hazardous substances regulation. It has identified a need for 25 codes of practice to assist compliance with hazardous substances regulation, but only 12 existed in the early 2010s, all of which the NZCIC had helped to frame relying on its own limited resources. It suggests that people in business are predisposed to do the right thing and follow what regulation expects them to do but that many business managers struggle with regulation that does not precisely define what is expected of them. They view it as primarily a government's responsibility to ensure that the implications of regulation are understood and that groups such as their own should be funded to help people and organizations meet regulatory requirements. Strong enforcement action to focus business managers on the need to address regulation is wanted. NZCIC points, for example, to regulation governing the carriage of dangerous goods. Initially of little impact, once it became possible to impose fines for separate transgressions connected to the same incident, NZCIC suggests business managers then started to take the regulation seriously. A single incident in which a truck was fined around NZ$60,000 (US$45,000) is said to have rapidly changed perceptions in the industry about the need to comply with the regulation.

Similarly, the possibility of banks acting as quasiregulators overlooks significant reasons to doubt that they would want or are able to perform such a role. Enforcement action brings a reputational risk for the bank as well as the client and may adversely affect customers' trust in an organization that appears to step outside its expected mandate. Moreover, in their relationship with commercial business, banks are primarily concerned with ensuring their clients remain financially strong, which may be expressed in minimizing discretionary actions beyond minimum compliance levels. On this basis, there is perhaps more prospect of insurance companies assisting regulators, because their interest in minimizing risk can align with that of regulators. A limitation is that the insurance is organized to accommodate a certain level of risk, and so, its incentive to enforce regulation cannot be relied upon entirely.

As noted in Chapter 2, the increased integration of much business activity within supply chains that are ultimately controlled by a comparatively small number of powerful, well-resourced organizations has been identified as offering a potential point of leverage for regulators. Consumer-facing organizations that are dependent on multitiered supply chains have already started to introduce environmental performance into their supply chain management. This is occurring voluntarily where supply chains stretch back to places with weak regulation, heightening the risks for the end supplier and where buyers are sensitive to the environmental performance of the organization they deal with. It has also been linked to the *clockspeed* of supply chains, referring to the rate at which supply chain relationships change.[21] The supply chain for personal computers, for example, has high clockspeed due to the frequency of product innovations. With high turnover in supply chain connections, it is potentially easier to introduce environmental performance considerations into supplier selection decisions than in a slow clockspeed industry. Where relationships are comparatively fixed, both parties may be required to move together, whereas with high clockspeed, the buyer has scope to unilaterally introduce additional demands on suppliers.

Regulation in a number of countries has taken advantage of the possibility of companies driving change through their supply chain connections by directly requiring traceability back to original sources of supply and by requiring original equipment manufacturers (OEMs) to manage their products when they become waste.[22] Because supply chains are extended to capture product disposal, take-back, and reuse, there is greater scope for a life cycle perspective to be brought into consideration than where OEM suppliers were concerned simply with the immediate impacts of their own operation. This is a promising development in stimulating better management of environmental impacts throughout the entire life of a service or product, but it may require further forms of regulatory intervention to realize the potential gains. Take-back obligations require firms to design and maintain collection networks, or at least ensure that these networks are in place. A constraint remains in the uncertainty around the volume, quality, and timing of used product collection and the ability to find uses for the recaptured and recycled materials. Thus, while the European Union's Waste Electrical and Electronics Equipment

(WEEE) regulation has been viewed as a welcome move toward encouraging "product stewardship," this approach currently works better for some forms of electrical device than others.[23]

Principle 5: Win–Win Outcomes are Encouraged Through Regulation

The original fifth principal for making smart regulation is "maximize opportunities for win–win outcomes." This has been modified in the light of the discussion in Chapter 1 that questioned the extent to which sustainability actions driven by a business case for action are actually delivering substantial "win–win" outcomes and the extent to which win–win opportunities arise independently of regulation. Both versions of the principle recognize that it is ideal to put in place circumstances in which businesses have an incentive to continuously improve their performance and that providing opportunities for business growth are effective ways of doing this.

Where regulation sets the context for voluntary action, there is more reason to think that voluntary action will produce significant steps toward a more sustainable future than where it is not supported by regulatory action. Broadly, regulation acts to economize more aspects of the natural environment in the sense that it requires that the use of environmental resources and services are more fully reflected in business decisions than they have been. This has two main outcomes. First, because more uses of the environment need to be paid for and previously free goods and services become another business cost, all businesses must give attention to more aspects of their environmental footprint. Second, it reduces impediments to being concerned with environmental performance as all businesses using the now to be paid for environmental services face a change in business costs. It can also mean that the financial returns are immediate and definite and are not reliant on appealing to a segment of consumers willing to respond to a product's or a service's environmental performance.

A difference between the original and reformulated principle is the question of defining a win, on both sides of the deal, but particularly qualifying what counts as an environmental gain. The discussion of win–win outcomes tends to not consider how wins are to be defined. This may not be too much of an issue with respect to business wins: these are generally agreed to be indicated by improvements in productivity and profitability, with ideally some consideration of the capacity to maintain performance as measured by a balanced scorecard. Environmental wins, on the other hand, are the subject of debate. Consider, for example, the following judgment that captures one aspect of the skepticism about the role that win–win opportunities have played so far.[24]

> Despite the very considerable advances in environmental man-agement over the last twenty years or so, planetary degradation has continued and, as far as any evidence suggests, no organiza-tion in its pursuit of eco-efficiency has succeeded in improving its eco-effectiveness...

The possibility of significant environmental improvement resulting as organizations identify a business case assumes the acceptability of incremental advancement, which essentially is the scope of ecoeffectiveness (see Chapter 1 for definitions of ecoefficiency and ecoeffectiveness). This form of improvement has a role to play and may merit recognition. Nonetheless, it needs to be considered whether the outcomes of incremental improvements are sufficient to justify impeding regulatory options and whether some effort is not needed to push the environmental wins in a preferred direction.

The linkage of win–win opportunities to regulation recognizes that there are limits to the improvement that business can justify through a case based on the financial returns that stand to be made. There are many environmental initiatives that a corporation is not going to put in place in the immediate future as they are simply not currently viable business options: zero waste, 100 percent renewable resource use, no impact on biodiversity, or operating within ecological footprint constraints. Leaders in sustainable business practice may espouse to achieve these things and seriously pursue them, but they are long-term goals that will impact on the state of the environment only if they are adopted and achieved by large number of businesses. Major changes in business behavior are going to be based on technological innovation, partly promoted through public support of R&D and coordinated investment in infrastructure to support shifts in energy, transport, and distribution systems. This indicates how more than regulation and business initiative alone are needed to deliver sustainable development.

Principle 6: Smart Regulation is Built Upon Smart Policy Evaluation

The need to give serious attention to policy evaluation forms part of the first principle, but it merits inclusion as a separate principle too. Proponents of the GRID, as discussed within Principle 1, argue that such methods can only be perfected through a willingness and ability to adapt regulation based on experience. In broad terms, few would doubt the importance of policy evaluation but the continued cases of policy failure suggest that there are barriers for doing this in practice. Connected to the political controversy that surrounds much regulation, it is possible to suggest a large number of reasons why policy evaluation falls short of what is required. Assuming the political will exists to support policy evaluation and there is openness to obtaining critical findings, issues still remain as to what form policy evaluation should take.

A danger of policy evaluation research is that the full mechanisms through which policy intervention can work are not known and that policy evaluation proceeds on the basis of an incomplete understanding of how businesses respond to the regulation. Experience with information sharing and emission trading indicates that this can occur. Taking the example of information sharing and the TRI, clearly the act of entering emissions data in a public register does not in itself lead to a reduction in emissions. If it does work, it must be through some consequence of the act of collecting and reporting emissions and through some processes in the minds of business decision makers and external parties able to influence the actions of business managers. As a tool for regulation, the TRI commenced with the understanding that information release was shocking and shaming high polluters to cutback their emissions. Subsequent evaluation raised doubts about this mechanism, identified alternative mechanisms through which emission reporting may change the effort to cutback emissions and identified conditions under which these various processes might operate. With the development of this insight, it is now possible to consider how information sharing might be deployed as an effective form of regulation. The careful elaboration of the mechanisms

Box 5.4 A Realist Evaluation of Gunpowder

Does gunpowder explode when a flame is applied to it? For a realist, the answer is yes if the conditions are right. Gunpowder that is wet does not ignite, if the mixture does not contain the right amounts of various elements, if oxygen is missing, or if the flame is withdrawn too quickly. In realist terms, the *outcome* (an explosion) of an *action* (applying the fame) follows from *mechanisms* (the chemical properties of the powder) acting in particular *contexts* (the conditions that enable the explosion).

through which regulation may affect change and the circumstances required for mechanisms to operate is a feature of *realist* approach to policy evaluation.[25] The simple example of gunpowder is often used to illustrate the principles of a realist approach to policy evaluation (Box 5.4).

An awareness that regulation operates through a mechanism that relies on supporting conditions can imply a different approach to policy evaluation than what is often taken to be the best way to evaluate policy intervention: the randomized control experiment. Where businesses are selected at random and divided according to their use of or exposure to a particular form of regulation there would seem to be a strong case for inferring any differences are a result of the regulation. This is the essence of a scientific approach to policy evaluation, but it is worth reflecting on how the scientific method works and what its shortcomings may be. Policy evaluation influenced by scientific research methods brings with it a particular understanding of what is needed to make a claim of causation or, in the context of policy research, a claim that a policy has worked. Science tends to follow a *successionist* logic whereas policy evaluation frequently would be better guided by a realist preference for *generative* logic.[26]

Successionists believe that causation is unobservable and that it is possible only to draw inferences on the basis of observational data. The key is to design a form of scientific inquiry that as far as possible controls for issues other than those that the investigation seeks to explore. According to successionists, some form of randomized allocation of subjects to experimental and control groups is the ideal way of making observations.

The assumption is that any difference in behavioral outcomes between the two groups is accounted for in terms of the action of the treatment, which in environmental policy might be participation in an emission trading program or the requirement to publicly release emission data. Causation is not observed but rather it is taken to exist if statistical analysis shows that the differences between the control and treatment groups are more than could be explained simply by chance. The outcome of successionist forms of inquiry tends to be the presentation of findings in the form of universal laws in the sense of them not being conditional on particular times or places. It tends to encourage what others have called "ontological universalism"[27] and what we may simply interpret as meaning that if a policy appears to have worked in one context it can be assumed to have equal chance of working in another, broadly similar context.

A generative view of causation seeks to establish a connection between action and outcomes in a way that gives a fuller explanation of how the two are linked. To this extent, it seeks to dig deeper into the process that causes change. A generative explanation makes reference to some underlying mechanism, which generates the connection and how the working of such mechanisms is contingent and conditional on particular contexts that allow the mechanisms to operate. A bias in favor of generative inquiry is consistent with the perception that events rarely have a single cause but are rather the result of a conjuncture of several factors or conditions.[28] A need for generative forms of explanation is especially called for when the issues of interest are part of the social rather than natural world. When seeking to understand processes involving events in the social world, there are many more things that can interfere with a supposed causal connection than when process can be studied in isolation from the particular context in which it occurs. An example of this may be seen in the way that insight into the operation of emission trading and information sharing has grown following detailed investigations that have revealed how outcomes have been a product of multiple conditions that cannot be certain to exist whenever the policy is attempted.

Clearly, the design of policy evaluation evolves more than simply the choice between a successionist and a generative logic, but the issue to which this connects is an important consideration. There are circumstances where a scientific approach to policy evaluation may be required and may yield valuable insight. It cannot be stated that smart regulation relies on generative logic but it can at least be argued that smart regulation is more likely to be developed where there is awareness of the different ways that evidence of policy effectiveness (or ineffectiveness) is recognized to exist than where the difference between successionist and generative logic is not recognized or not thought to be important.

Chapter Summary

Normative policy choices attempt to match the environmental issue with the best available policy approach. A political economy perspective on policy selection emphasizes institutional and political pressures that change the interpretation of different policy approaches based on shifts in perceived effectiveness. The normative interpretation encourages policy makers to select from a broad menu of regulatory options. The political economy interpretation implies that policy selections are informed by political considerations rather than evidence of their greater effectiveness than alternative policy selections. Both interpretations mean that policy managers should make case-by-case policy decisions rather than be guided by a default best option. Rather than a particular form of policy design, smart regulation is based on applying five principles of regulatory design. This chapter has summarized the principles as: (i) utilize a mix of regulatory styles rather than a single form of regulation; (ii) minimize the extent of intervention; (iii) build responsiveness into policy programs; (iv) maximize the use of nongovernmental regulators; (v) win–win outcomes are encouraged through regulation; and (vi) smart regulation is built upon smart policy evaluation.

Key Concepts

Circuit breaker: a short-term measure to overcome opposition or other impediments to the use of another instruments that ultimately is the preferred approach for dealing with the issue.

Clockspeed: the frequency with which end buyers in supply chains change their supply relationships.

Coercive regulation: regulation with power to enforce or compel compliance among entities covered by the regulation.

Generative logic: a view of causation that holds there is a need to identify a specific mechanism linking causes to change. Applied to policy evaluation, a generative logic holds that regulation brings a potential to change the behavior of economic actors, whether change occurs depends on conditions and circumstances.

Good regulatory intervention design (GRID): a hybrid style of regulation that combines elements of risk and responsive forms of regulation.

Good Regulatory Assessment Framework (GRAF): a systematic evaluation to investigate the performance of the GRID.

Hybrid regulation: regulation design based on a mix of two or more types of regulation, for example, the mixing of risk and responsive regulation to create a single style.

Intervention: measured by the level of prescription and coercion associated with a form of regulation.

Normative guidance: applied to policy selection, the way policy is chosen according to an understanding of which policy instrument is likely to be most effective in addressing the issue of concern.

Political economy: applied to policy selection, an interpretation focused on the competition among competing interest groups and the considerations influencing different groups' assessment of policy choices.

Prescriptive intervention: measured by the extent to which regulation gives options as to how to comply; prescriptive regulation gives few options as to the action expected to be taken.

Quasiregulators: nongovernment agencies enlisted to assist public agencies gain compliance to regulation.

Randomized control experiment: an approach to policy evaluation based on comparing outcomes between groups that are randomly selected from those affected and not affected by the policy intervention.

Realism: a model of scientific explanation that believes it is possible and necessary to specify how variables in a cause and effect relationship are connected by reference to the mechanism and context that connects them. This differs from models of scientific explanation that infer causation by observing changes in the variables that are thought to be potentially linked.

Really responsive regulation: regulation that is responsive to the capacity of the agency, the culture of the sector being regulated, the performance of the regulation, and how the significance and performance of regulation is affected by changes in the overall economic and political environment.

Successionist logic: a view of causation that supports the use of control groups for measuring the impact of intervention. Applied to policy intervention, effectiveness is judged by comparing similar groups of enterprises with one group affected by regulation and one group not affected.

Trigger: a threshold level (for example, the volume of emissions or number of organizations implementing environmental management systems) that indicates a need to commence a more interventionist form of regulation.

Endnotes

1. Gunningham *et al.* (1999).
2. Stavins (2003).
3. Sterner and Coria (2012).
4. Table based on OECD (2010), p. 6; de Freitas and Perry (2012) Table 2.4.
5. Stavins (2003).
6. For an explanation of industry representation, see Olson (1971), and for more contemporary application, see Barnett (2006); Battisti and Perry (2015).
7. Jaffe *et al.* (1995).
8. Gunningham *et al.* (1999).
9. Gunningham *et al.* (1999).
10. Gunningham *et al.* (1999), pp. 422–53.
11. Black and Baldwin (2012).
12. The figure is based on Baldwin *et al.* (2013), p. 10.
13. Baldwin *et al.* (2013), p. 21.

14. Black and Baldwin (2010).

15. Sterner (2003), p. 365.

16. Lindhqvist (2000), p. 88.

17. Gunningham *et al.* (1999), p. 408.

18. See Perry (2010) for a discussion of this in Australia and New Zealand; Bennett and Ramsden (2007) for the UK; and Barnett (2006) for the United States.

19. For an explanation of the recruitment challenge faced by trade associations, see Perry (2009).

20. This case draws on an interview conducted by Martin Perry with representatives of the NZCIC in 2011. The organization is now known as Responsible Care New Zealand, see www.nzcic.org.nz

21. Vachon *et al.* (2009).

22. See Klassen and Vachon (2012); Lehmann and Crocker (2012).

23. See discussion in Lehmann and Crocker (2012).

24. Buhr and Gray (2012), p. 437.

25. See Pawson and Tilley (1997) for an introduction to realist policy evaluation.

26. For an elaboration see Pawson and Tilley (1997); Robson (2002); and Perry (2010).

27. Kenny and Williams (2001), p. 3.

28. Kenny and Williams (2001), p. 13.

CHAPTER 6

Implications for Managers

This guide to environmental regulation for business has identified a growing agenda of policy options. It has discussed a search for alternative styles of regulation that attend to concerns that regulators as well as the regulated have with the traditional, standard-based ways of designing regulation. The broad impact of traditional regulation was to provide regulated parties with comparatively little discretion over what they must do to meet the goals set by the regulator. There can be merit in this approach as when there is a need to remove a toxic material from use or there is a need to safeguard human populations and ecosystems from serious and immediate harm. Contemporary environmental policy still has these concerns, but it also has a broadened agenda of seeking to promote sustainable forms of development. Sustainability is a more ambitious policy target than simply protecting people and places from imminent and certain sources of harm. Policy goals such as encouraging more businesses to adopt green technologies, generate less waste, and convert to renewable resources are best pursued in ways that give at least some discretion to the subjects of regulation to set their own means of responding to the issue and their own policy targets.

The shift in policy toward more discretion is variously a response to a belief that people and organizations will be motivated to pursue issues, beyond that which a regulatory agency (and public attitudes) might consider reasonable to enforce, the difficulty of specifying what action needs to be taken when this is partly a matter of individual opportunity and the ability to pursue some policy targets based on the aggregate performance of an industry or other collective grouping rather than the performance of each and every industry participant. The concern of this chapter is to identify some of the implications of the shift toward more discretionary styles of regulation. This commences by outlining a framework to distinguish regulation according to two aspects of discretion that may assist managers identify a preferred approach. For organizations supporting the shift to more discretionary forms of regulation while aspiring to be recognized as responsible enterprises and as leaders in the shift to a more sustainable economy, this chapter offers five points to consider about the fit between responsible management and discretionary styles of regulation.

A Framework for Mapping Policy Choices

While the general direction of innovation in regulation has been to provide regulated parties with more discretion, this occurs in different ways and to different degrees. A way of simplifying the new forms of regulation is to distinguish the two main aspects of regulation over which discretion may be given: how far regulation mandates a specific level of performance (*performance discretion*) and how much discretion is provided to individual businesses to determine how to comply with the regulation (*action discretion*) (Figure 6.1). Action discretion concerns the extent to which regulation proscribes an expected course of action (low discretion) when compared with regulation setting broad outcomes to be attained without specifying how this outcome is to be achieved (high discretion). Performance discretion measures the extent to which the type of regulation typically sets a specified level of performance that all regulated entities are required to attain. These two factors are likely to be among the considerations informing a manager's assessment of the burden imposed by regulation although with different perspectives whether performance and action discretion are preferred over regulation that specifies what regulated parties are expected to do and how far they are expected to go (see discussion of responsive regulation in Chapter 2).

The framework recognizes that regulation which provides business with a high degree of discretion in how to respond may not set a specific performance level to be attained: an example being information sharing, which specifies the form of information to be shared and how it is to be shared but can leave it to the discretion of a business as to how they respond. Conversely, regulation that gives businesses little discretion in how to respond may not set a specific performance level to be attained: examples of this are command and control with process standards (C&C

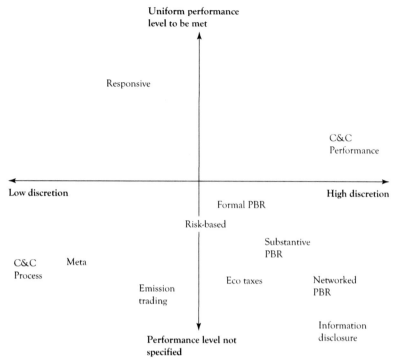

Figure 6.1 Mapping regulatory options according to levels of discretion

process in Figure 6.1) and metaregulation where the focus is on specifying a management process to be followed rather than the level of performance that results from that process. With metaregulation, for example,
the management process to be followed can be specified in such detail as
to effectively ensure a minimum level of performance, but the essence of
this form of regulation is that it preserves a high degree of operational
discretion to determine what level of performance is attained.[1] As discussed in Chapter 2, regulators may judge that allowing individual entities to set their own performance level is the best approach when they are
faced with an issue over which they have little understanding or which
is subject to high variability between regulated parties. In such circumstances, regulators may judge that it is most practical to limit their role to
monitoring control plans and management systems rather than enforcing
performance levels.

The mapping of the main types of regulation indicates a concentration of regulation that is comparatively high in discretion and low in performance specification. This is consistent with the thinking informing the development of the so-called new governance techniques where the emphasis has been on moving away from the use of uniform standards across all aspects of regulation.[2] As in the case of environmental policy making, this is part of a "better regulation" movement that seeks to minimize the perceived burden of regulation on business but it has other justifications too. Where regulators find themselves at an information disadvantage compared with the parties being overseen, there is a general case for designing regulation that can put pressure on regulated parties to regulate themselves.

As with information-based regulation, each type of regulation has a characteristic degree of action and performance discretion but the precise design and context in which regulation is applied can affect how regulation works in practice. For example, as discussed in Chapter 2, formal PBR can resemble command and control regulation where principles are expressed in such detail that they effectively enforce a uniform performance expectation. The value of the discretion-based framework is in pointing managers to a style of regulation that can match their preference for determining their own action and performance. Some managers may favor the new styles of regulation that maximize individual discretion and avoid uniform performance standards, whereas others may prefer the uniformity that results from the lack of discretion and setting of a specific level of performance. This may be a question of organizational capacity and confidence to deal with regulation: in organizations with limited resources and little experience of addressing environmental concerns, there may be a preference for regulation that gives precise instruction on what businesses are expected to do. This is connected to the way managers can be expected to vary in their concern about how regulation may affect market competition. Among smaller companies, it has been highlighted how a concern that regulation is not enforced consistently encourages support for command and control approaches over those that permit more discretion to be exercised.[3]

The perceived need for and effectiveness of environmental regulation is a further consideration affecting the outlook of management. The kind of proactive response looked for when firms set their own course of action implies that managers accept the need for change. The willingness of business organizations to regulate themselves, as required where there is high discretion and no set performance level, is dependent on managers seeing a need for the regulation based on acceptance of the underlying issue and on managers believing that the regulation is an effective response. Clearly, the growth of business interest in environmental sustainability and social responsibility indicates that many companies are taking action to improve their performance. Nonetheless, a number of issues need to be considered before concluding that discretionary forms of regulation and responsible management are aligned in the interests of building a more sustainable world.

Questions for Responsible Management

Shifting discretion over how to regulate from regulators to the target of regulation is justified where this produces better outcomes more efficiently than where the regulator enforces rules. These better outcomes are possible where the targets of regulation have greater knowledge of and information about their own operations in ways that affect the ability to determine the optimal steps that need to be taken to secure the objectives of regulation.[4] Further, discretion can be justified where it makes the need for change seem more reasonable than change required to meet externally imposed rules and, in turn, this brings a greater motivation to make the change. A caveat is that devolving some of the responsibility for regulation, which implies that regulators lose some of their control over each and every regulated party, is not an option where it is important to ensure that all regulated parties are taking steps to address the issue of regulatory concern. For responsible business organizations wishing to be viewed as leaders in corporate responsibility and for the community around them supporting this endeavor (industry associations, business advocacy groups, and consultants), the shift to discretionary styles of regulation is an opportunity to continue with individual initiatives. It also implies a need to consider the implications for management of operating in a context where they are expected to regulate themselves rather than follow prescriptive instructions. Five questions to be considered are discussed below.

Does your business environment suit
discretionary regulation?

The framework mapping regulatory options may assist managers identify
a preferred style of regulation according to their preference for discretion
and performance flexibility, but the conditions in which different styles of
regulation are designed to operate need to be considered too. Regulators'
preference for a particular form of regulation is guided by an understanding of its fit with the nature of the environmental issue being addressed
and the business environment in which it is to be applied. As discussed in
Chapter 5, policy choices are affected by institutional pressures that can
result in policy approaches being tried in circumstances to which they are
not well suited. Nonetheless, ultimately normative considerations shaping
policy effectiveness will influence the use of different forms of regulation.

Recognizing that regulation needs to fit the context in which it is applied, advocates of discretionary regulation can strengthen their case by
showing its appropriateness to the business environment in which it will
be applied. A poor fit risks rendering policy intervention ineffective or inefficient or both and may involve a waste of time and resources in adjusting to regulation that is ultimately found to be in need of replacement.
Within any style of regulation there is capacity for some adjustment to
suit the particular context in which it is applied (see discussion of the use
of the GRID in Chapter 2), but it is also possible to provide some general
guidance about the business conditions to which different styles of regulation are best targeted (Table 6.1). This information sits alongside the
normative guidance to policy selection that was discussed in Chapter 5.
That information is concerned with how the nature of environmental issues can inform policy selection: here the concern is with identifying how
the nature of the business environment can affect the choice of regulation.

The styles of policy that are based on comparatively high levels of
discretion and that allow business to set their own performance level are
premised on the assumption that the targets of regulation have far more
insight into and information about their own operations than regulators
could readily obtain. This may arise when regulators lack the resources or
information to devise performance or process standards to cover issues
that are highly variable between organizations and over time or when a

Table 6.1 Business environments for regulation

Regulation design and assumption of business behavior	Assumptions about the business environment
Command and control performance standard	All regulated businesses have a similar opportunity to meet a specified performance level. A standard technological solution can be applied by all businesses to meet the performance standard.
Command and control process standard	A standard set of work practices can be adopted and applied by all types of business in all types of work situation.
Responsive	Business is generally supportive of the regulation and sees it in their best interests to cooperate with the goals of regulation. Managers have confidence that enforcement action will be taken against noncomplying businesses.
Risk-based	Environmental risks are well understood with business assisting regulators identify levels of risk.
Principle-based	There is considerable variability among businesses in terms of the nature of environmental risks they pose and the means for minimizing those risks. Regulated parties are prepared to engage in discussions with regulators, industry groups, and third parties over the ways to put principles into practice. Business responds to the freedom to work out their own way of complying by setting challenging performance goals and making progress in attaining them.
Meta	Environmental risks are contingent upon individual circumstances, for example, varying with the precise mix and volumes of toxic materials handled. Regulated parties have insight into and knowledge about the environmental impacts and risks of their activities that is not readily communicated to outside parties. Business is more committed to meeting internally set performance goals than performance goals set by a regulator.
Taxation	Liability for financial payments stimulates the adoption of alternatives practices to avoid payment.
Emissions trading	Businesses are differently positioned to adopt environmentally preferred technologies but financial incentives can ensure sufficient change is realized to achieve environmental targets for an industry as a whole.
Information disclosure	The collection of information has the potential to provide new insight into how to minimize or eradicate environmental impacts that businesses act upon. Businesses are sensitive to public perception of their environmental performance and act to avoid being viewed as a laggard in terms of their environmental performance.

problem or the potential existence of a problem is not well understood by outside regulators. In such circumstances, business managers are more likely to be in a position to find the most cost-effective solution to the problem or issue than is a regulator. Knowing that they have this insight can make managers and employees in organizations resistant to regulation that is designed without sensitivity to individual circumstances. In this context, allowing organizations some freedom to set their own rules and control processes can make regulation seem more reasonable than a command and control approach, and, in turn, this can lead to high levels of compliance.

Responsible business seeking to encourage the use of regulation with action and performance discretion can help demonstrate ther acceptability of this by showing how the assumptions on which the regulation is founded are met and that they recognize how the regulation expects them to behave. The acid test of the effectiveness of allowing discretion is that the freedom to determine what to do and how far to go is used to good effect and not simply to evade less permissive styles of regulation. In broad terms, this can be understood as a need for responsible business to demonstrate that discretion encourages them to search for better outcomes than could be achieved by imposing standardized solutions on business.

Are You Willing To Look Beyond Market-Based Regulation?

The debate around corporate responsibility and regulation has been framed mainly in terms of a choice between command and control and market-based instruments. This is partly because the shift away from traditional standards-based regulation has so far been dominated by market-based approaches. Market-based tools can be effective and can impose significant constraints on business, but when combined with the ability to engage in environment benefit trading or offsetting, they can be comparatively undemanding on business and not particularly effective at addressing the issue that they were introduced in response to. It can be assumed that business would react differently to emissions trading schemes that imposed tight emission caps designed to force the pace of technological change and that limit the scope for offsetting emissions as an alternative to cutting them at source. Similarly, although initially claimed as an example of successful regulation, the achievements of the Toxics Release Inventory have been questioned partly on the grounds that the data collection procedures to be followed were not sufficiently specified or monitored (see Chapter 3). With the case for market-based instruments still open to debate and with their lack of suitability to some types of environmental issue, other styles of regulation will need to be tried if discretion is to remain a consideration. Metaregulation and principle-based regulation have potential to play a role, but it is not yet established that business is prepared to commit to these approaches, but this is partly because their use remains comparatively rare. As a first step, the responsible business community could help raise awareness of their possible application and educate managers about their potential implications.

Is Discretionary Regulation Consistent With Enterprise Thinking?

One of the hallmarks of responsible management is frequently taken to be the willingness to behave as an extended enterprise (see Chapter 1) and engage in *enterprise thinking*.[5] This means the willingness to search for solutions across the industry as a whole, encompassing suppliers and customers rather than simply seeking to improve your own enterprise's performance. The logic for this is that there is more scope for significant improvement if the interests of an individual enterprise are not allowed to restrict the scope of change. This form of enterprise thinking has application to the shift in regulation too. A responsible business has opportunity to demonstrate that they have considered how the adoption of discretionary regulation affects the business community as a whole rather than simply considering their individual situation. As noted in the context of the framework mapping regulatory options, businesses are likely to differ in their assessment of regulation partly according to their ability to deal with and the perceived benefit obtained from high levels of discretion. In this context, a responsible business can show its commitment to addressing the issue attracting regulation by showing that its preferred way of addressing the issue in terms of high or low discretion forms of regulation is best for the industry as a whole. Of course, understanding and managing the burden of regulation is partly the job of regulatory agencies, but this does not have to preclude business also demonstrating awareness of how a particular style of regulation may favor some types of business over others.

How Do You Go Beyond Compliance?

The willingness to go *beyond compliance* is frequently claimed to be an aspect of a responsible business. Going beyond compliance ensures that there is always a margin of difference between what regulation requires a business to do and the standards that business attains. Staying ahead of regulation, it is argued, minimizes the risk of being found to be noncompliant should your performance slip or expectations suddenly change, puts you on good terms with regulators, and gives other reputational gains. Moreover, it makes sense to be ahead of regulation where it can be expected that the standards demanded by regulators are likely to be raised as part of society's growing concern to protect the environment.

Judging what actions represent going beyond compliance is not always straightforward. Where regulation mandates a performance or process standard this can be used as a benchmark against which an organization's performance can be compared. New approaches to environmental regulation tend to provide no clear performance benchmark from which a claim of going beyond compliance can be justified. It clearly requires that regulated parties share the goals of public regulatory agencies in bringing an issue under control, as well as encouraging further reflection on the role of regulation, by giving attention to how regulation is intended to work it is possible to be specific about what it means to go "beyond compliance." Rather than simply thinking in terms of putting the organization beyond risk of being noncompliant, different forms of regulation can afford different ways of demonstrating a business's willingness to go beyond compliance.

In the context of information sharing, for example, one form of going beyond compliance is to produce an environmental report that meets the guidelines set by the Global Reporting Initiative. A comprehensive, GRI-compliant environmental report shows respect for the right of the public to know about a business's environmental performance. Another form of going beyond compliance would be to show that the act of producing an environmental report is having an impact and bringing benefits as intended by the reasons for wanting information to be shared. As discussed in Chapter 3, a number of mechanisms exist through which information sharing may bring benefits: publishing an environmental report does not in itself demonstrate these benefits are being obtained. To do this, an organization could explain what has been learnt from the data collected as part of its information sharing, how this has given it new insights, and how behavior is changing as a consequence. As with other performance reporting, demonstrating improvement above that which would occur through the normal process of new investment is a further way for responsible businesses to justify a claim of going beyond compliance.

In the case of emission trading, the goal is to encourage the transition to a preferred technology and to retire activity associated with negative environmental outcomes. In trading schemes that include the use of offsets, a responsible business seeking to claim it is going beyond compliance could show this by establishing how it has accelerated out of the technology that regulation is aiming to reduce. Principle-based regulation requires that regulated parties help develop understanding of how the broad goals of the principles to be followed can be translated into specific actions. This implies a willingness to support and participate in industry dialog and to recognize the role of industry and other bodies to help translate principles into an agreed understanding of how they are to be applied. In the case of metaregulation going beyond compliance can involve integrating the required management systems into core management processes rather than simply implementing them as a parallel set of procedures. Demonstrating that management systems are updated in line with the changing circumstances of the organization is another way for a commitment to go beyond compliance to be demonstrated with this particular form of regulation.

Does Discretionary Regulation Result In Innovation?

Ultimately, regulation applied to the goal of improving the state of the environment and of encouraging the adoption of sustainable technologies, whatever form it takes, should play some role in stimulating innovation that reduces if not evades the need for regulation. Going back to the example of smart regulation discussed in Chapter 1, the top runner program combined positive and negative incentives to simultaneously discourage environmentally damaging activity and stimulate the move to better environmental options. This combination of outcomes is certainly an aspect of smart regulation (as reflected in Principle 5 and the use of circuit breakers as part of Principle 3), but one of the potential risks of moving away from command and control styles of regulation is that this incentive reduces. It has been pointed out that one of the strengths of traditional regulation based on uniform standards is that it requires businesses to respond in comparatively uniform ways.[6] As a consequence, this helps to build a market for pollution control equipment, green technologies, and environmental services that help business meet the requirements of regulation. The comparative ease of monitoring compliance and enforcing standard-based regulation helps to encourage the demand for these environmental technologies.

A criticism of market-based approaches, as discussed in Chapter 4, is that by allowing the purchase of emission credits they provide an alternative to investing in abatement technologies or truly green technologies. A well-designed emission trading scheme may minimize the incentive to avoid taking measures to improve, but a lesson from the recent experience of emission trading for greenhouse gases is that good design can be hard to achieve. Other alternatives to command and control styles of regulation have yet to be tested in terms of their role in encouraging innovation and until this is proved managers seeking discretion in how they respond to regulatory concerns should be expected to show that their preferred style of regulation will help to bring forward the kinds of ecoeffective solutions needed for a sustainable economy.

Chapter Summary

Different approaches to regulation can be distinguished according to the level of performance and action discretion that they permit. Newer styles of regulation tend to be high in both performance and action discretion. The shift to discretionary styles of regulation is an aspect of the broadening scope of environmental policy to encompass sustainability, and it can be viewed as broadly consistent with the proactive actions of responsible business organizations. Five questions that responsible business organizations can ask about the use of discretionary regulation are: (1) Is your business environment right for discretionary regulation? (2) Are you willing to look beyond market-based regulation? (3) Is discretionary regulation consistent with enterprise thinking? (4) How do you go beyond compliance? (5) Does discretionary regulation result in innovation?

Key Concepts

Action discretion: the freedom to determine how to respond to meet the requirements of regulation, such as whether to invest in pollution control equipment or whether to reduce the generation of pollution.

Beyond compliance: setting performance goals and achieving levels of performance that exceed those required by regulation.

Enterprise thinking:—the willingness to search for solutions by engaging with all related businesses to find the best alternatives rather than restricting the search for improvement to that which your own enterprise can achieve alone.

Performance discretion: the freedom to determine the level of performance rather than being required to achieve a performance level set by regulation, such as the energy efficiency of products produced or volume of waste generated.

Endnotes

1. See Goglianese and Mendelson (2010) for a full explanation of discretion and metaregulation.
2. Baldwin (2010) provides a summary of the reasons for reforming regulation.
3. Petts (2000).
4. See Goglianese and Mendelson (2010) for a full explanation of this.
5. Rainey (2005).
6. Driesen (2010), p. 2.

References

Agency for Natural Resources and Energy, Ministry of Economy, Trade and Industry (2010) Top Runner Program: Developing the World's Best Energy Efficiency Appliances. Tokyo: ANRE/METI.

Ali, S. (2009) Treasurers of the Earth. New Haven: Yale University Press.

Amodu, T. (2008) The Determinants of Compliance with Laws and Regulations with Special Reference to Health and Safety: A Literature Review. Report for the UK Health and Safety Executive, Research Report RR638. Online at: http://www.hse.gov.uk/research/rrpdf/rr638.pdf

Andersen, M. (1994) Governance by Green Taxes: Making Pollution Prevention Pay. Manchester: Manchester University Press.

Arnold, F.S. (1995) Economic Analysis of Environmental Policy and Regulations. New York: John Wiley & Sons.

Ashford, N. (1997) Industrial safety: the neglected issue in industrial ecology. Journal of Cleaner Production, 5(1-2): 115-21.

Baldwin, R. (1997) Regulation after command and control. In K. Hawkins (ed.) The Human Face of Law: Essays in Honour of Donald Harris. Oxford: Oxford University Press.

Baldwin, R. (2010) Better regulation: the search and the struggle. In R. Baldwin, M. Cave and M. Lodge (eds.) The Oxford Handbook of Regulation. Oxford Handbooks Online: www.oxfordhandbooks.com

Baldwin, R. and Black, J. (2008) Really responsive regulation. Modern Law Review, 71(1): 59-94.

Baldwin, R., Black, J. and O'Leary, G. (2013) Regulating low risks: innovative strategies and implementation. LSE Law, Society and Economy Working Papers 9/2013, London School of Economics and Political Science Law Department.

Barham, E. (2003) Translating terroir: the global challenge of French AOC labeling. Journal of Rural Studies, 19: 127-38.

Barnett, M. (2006) Finding a working balance between competitive and communal strategies. Journal of Management Studies, 438: 1753-73.

Barrow C. J. (2006) Environmental Management for Sustainable Development, 2nd edition. London: Routledge.

Battisti, M. and Perry, M. (2015) Small enterprise affiliations to business associations and the collective action problem revisited. Small Business Economics. 44(3): 559-76

Beierle, T. (2003) The benefits and costs of environmental information disclosure: what do we know about right-to-know? Resources for the Future Discussion Paper 03-05. Washington, DC: Resources for the Future.

Bennett, R. and Ramsden, M. (2007) The contribution of business associations to SMEs: strategy, bundling or reassurance? International Small Business Journal, 251: 49-76.

Better Regulation Task Force (2000) Alternatives to State Regulation. London: Cabinet Office Publications and Publicity Team.

Black, J. (2002) Decentring regulation: understanding the role of regulation and self regulation in a 'post-regulatory' world. Current Legal Problems, 54(1): 10346.

Black, J. (2008) Forms and paradoxes of principles based regulation. Capital Markets Law Journal, 3(4): 42557.

Black, J. (2014) Learning from regulatory disasters. Sir Frank Holmes Memorial Lecture April 2014. Wellington: Victoria University of Wellington.

Black, J. and Baldwin, R. (2010) Really responsive risk-based regulation. Law and Policy, 32(2): 181-213.

Black, J. and Baldwin, R. (2012) When risk-based regulation aims low, Part I: approaches and challenges. Regulation and Governance, 6(1): 1-21.

Black, J., Lodge, M. and Thatcher, M. (2005) Regulatory Innovation: A Comparative Analysis. Cheltenham: Edward Elgar.

Blowfield, M. and Murray, A. (2008) Corporate Responsibility: A Critical Introduction. Oxford: Oxford University Press.

Boyd, E. (2009) Governing the clean development mechanism: global rhetoric versus local realities in carbon sequestration projects. Environment and Planning A, 41: 2380-95.

Boyd E., Grist, N., Juhola, S. and Nelson, V. (2009) Exploring development futures in a changing climate: frontiers for development policy and practice. Development Policy Review, 27(6): 659-74.

Boyfield, K. (2009) Cure or Disease? The Unintended Consequences of Regulation. Adam Smith Institute, Briefing Paper. Online at: http://adamsmith.org/images/stories/unintended-consequences.pdf

Braithwaite, J. (1993) Responsive business regulatory institutions. In C. Cody and C. Stampford (eds.) Business, Ethics, and Law. Sydney: Federation Press.

Braithwaite, J. (2008) Regulatory Capitalism: How it Works, Ideas for Making it Work Better. Cheltenham: Edward Elgar.

Braithwaite, J. and Drahos, P. (2000) Global Business Regulation. Cambridge: Cambridge University Press.

Better Regulation Executive (BRE) (2009) Better Regulation, Better Benefits: Getting the Balance Right, Main Report. Online at: http://www.berr.gov.uk/files/file53252.pdf

Buhr, N. and Gray, R. (2012) Environmental management, measurement, and accounting: information for decision and control? In P. Bansal and A. Hoffman (eds.) The Oxford Handbook of Business and the Natural Environment. Oxford: Oxford University Press.

Cho, C., Patten, D. and Roberts, R. (2012) Corporate environmental financial reporting and financial markets. In P. Bansal and A. Hoffman (eds.) The Oxford Handbook of Business and the Natural Environment. Oxford: Oxford University Press.

Coglianese, C. (2009) Engaging business in the regulation of nanotechnology. In C. Bosso (ed.) Environmental Regulation in the Shadow of Nanotechnology: Confronting Conditions of Uncertainty. Baltimore: John Hopkins University/Resources for the Future Press.

Coglianese, C. and Mendelson, D. (2010) Meta regulation and self-regulation. In R. Baldwin, M. Cave and M. Lodge (eds.) The Oxford Handbook of Regulation. Oxford Handbooks Online: www.oxfordhandbooks.com

Cohen, S. (2014) Understanding Environmental Policy. New York: Columbia University Press.

Cohen-Rosenthal, E. (2003) What is eco-industrial development? In E. Cohen-Rosenthal (ed.) Eco-industrial Strategies. Sheffield: Greenleaf.

Congressional Budget Office (2000) Who gains and who pays under carbon-allowance trading? The distributional effects of alternative policy designs. Washington, DC: Congressional Budget Office.

Corbera, E. and Brown, K. (2010) Offsetting benefits? Analyzing access to forest carbon. Environment and Planning A, 42(7): 1739-61.

Corbera, E., Estrada, M. and Brown, K. (2009) How do regulated and voluntary carbon-offset schemes compare? Journal of Integrative Environmental Sciences, 6(1):26-50.

Daly, H. (1990) Toward some operational principles of sustainable development. Ecological Economics, 2: 1-6.

Daly, H. (1996) Beyond Growth: The Economics of Sustainable Development. Boston: Beacon Press.

Dauvergne, P. (2008) Shadows of Consumption. Boston: MIT Press.

Dauvergne, P. and Lister, J. (2013) Eco Business. Boston: MIT Press.

de Freitas, C. and Perry, M. (2012) New Environmentalism: Managing New Zealand's Environmental Diversity. Dordrecht: Springer.

Driesen, D. (1998) Fee lunch or cheap fix? The emission trading idea and the climate change convention. Boston College Environmental Law Review, 26(1): 66-67.

Driesen, D. (2010) Alternatives to regulation? Market mechanisms and the environment. In R. Baldwin, M. Cave and M. Lodge (eds.) The Oxford Handbook of Regulation. Oxford Handbooks Online: www.oxfordhandbooks.com

Driesen, D. and Ghosh, S. (2005) The function of transaction costs: rethinking transaction cost minimization in a world of friction. Arizona Law Review, 47(1): 61-111.

Environmental Data Services (2005) Two decades of responsible care: Credible response or comfort blanket? ENDS Report 360. London: Environmental Data Services (ENDS) Ltd.

ENTEC UK (2003) Costs of compliance with health and safety regulations in SME's. Report for the UK Health and Safety Executive. Online at: http://www.hse.gov.uk/research/rrpdf/rr174.pdf

EPA (2013) The Toxics Release Inventory in Action: Media, Government, Business, Community and Academic Uses of TRI Data. Washington DC: US Environmental Protection Agency.

Epstein, M. (2008) Making Sustainability Work. Sheffield: Greenleaf.

Esty, D. and Porter, M. (1998) Industrial ecology and competitiveness. Journal of Industrial Ecology, 2(1): 35-43.

Esty, D. and Winston, A. (2006) From Green to Gold: How Smart Companies Use Environmental Strategy to Innovate. New York: Wiley.

Fairtrade Foundation (2008) Tipping the Balance: The Fairtrade Foundation's Vision for Transforming Trade, 2008-2012. London: The Fairtrade Foundation.

Fifield, A. (2010) Evangelist in sheep's clothing. Financial Times, June 2. Online: http://www.ft.com/intl/cms/s/0/f70ed46c-6ddd-11df-b5c9-00144feabdc0.html#axzz3VQREMaTy

Fresh Minds (2009) The Benefits of Regulation: A Public and Business Perceptions Study, URN 09/1403. Online at: http://www.berr.gov.uk/files/file53236.pdf

Fung, A. and O'Rourke, D. (2000) Reinventing environmental regulation from the grassroots up: explaining and expanding the success of the toxics release inventory. Environmental Management, 25(2): 115-27.

Gibbs, D. and Deutz, P. (2005) Implementing industrial ecology? Planning for eco-industrial parks in the USA. Geoforum, 36: 452-64.

Gorenak, S. and Bobek, Y. (2010) Total responsibility management indicators and sustainable development. International Journal of Sustainable Society, 2(3): 248-64.

Goulder, L.H. (2000) Confronting the adverse industry impacts of carbon dioxide abatement policies: What does it cost? Resources for the Future Issues Brief 23. Washington, DC: Resources for the Future.

Gouldson, A. and Murphy, J. (1996) Ecological modernization and the European Union. Geoforum, 27: 11-21.

Gouldson, A., Murphy, J. (1998) Regulatory realities: the implementation and impact of industrial environmental regulation. London: Earthscan Publications.

Graham, M. and Millar, C. (2001) Disclosure of toxic releases in the United States. Environment, 43(8): 11-23.

Gray, R. and Herremans, I. (2012) Sustainability and social responsibility reporting and the emergence of the external social audits: the struggle for accountability. In P. Bansal and A. Hoffman (eds.) The Oxford Handbook of Business and the Natural Environment. Oxford: Oxford University Press.

Gunningham, N., Grabosky, P. and Sinclair, D. (1999) Smart Regulation: Designing Environmental Policy. Oxford: Oxford University Press.

Gunningham, N., Kaga, R. and Thornton, D. (2004) Social license and environmental protection: why businesses go beyond compliance. Law and Social Inquiry, 29: 307-41.

Haigh, N. and Irwin, F. (1990) Integrated Pollution Control in Europe and North America. Washington, DC: The Conservation Foundation.

Haines, F. (1997) Corporate Regulation: Beyond 'Punish or Persuade'. Oxford: Clarendon Press.

Haines, F. (2011) The Paradox of Regulation: What Regulation Can Achieve and What It Cannot. Cheltenham: Edward Elgar.

Harris, L. (2002) Small Firm Responses to Employment Regulation. Journal of Small Business and Enterprise Development, 9(3): 296-306.

Harrison, K. and Antweiler, W. (2001) Toxic release inventories and green consumerism: empirical evidence from Canada. Canadian Journal of Economics/Revue canadienne d'économique, 36(2): 495-520.

Hillary, R. (2000) ISO14001 case studies of practical experiences. Sheffield: Greenleaf.

Hoffman, A. (2005) Climate change strategy: the business logic behind voluntary greenhouse gas reductions. California Management Review, 47(3): 21-46.

Hoffman, A. and Bansal, P. (2012) Retrospective, perspective, and prospective: introduction to the Oxford handbook on business and the natural environment. In P. Bansal and A. Hoffman (eds.) The Oxford Handbook of Business and the Natural Environment. Oxford: Oxford University Press.

Huber, J. (1985) The Rainbow Society: Ecology and Social Politics. Frankfurt am Main: Fisher Verlag.

ISO (2011) The ISO Survey—2011. Geneva: ISO. Online at: www.iso.org

Jaffe, A., Peterson, S., Portney, P. and Stavins, R. (1995) Environmental regulation and the competitiveness of US manufacturing: what does the evidence tell us? Journal of Economic Literature, 33(1): 132-63.

Jänicke, M. (1985) Preventive Environmental Policy as Ecological Modernization and Structural Policy, Discussion Paper IIUG dp85-2. Internationales Institut Für Umwelt und Gesellschaft, Wissenschaftszentrum Berlin Für Sozialforschung.

Jänicke, M. (2008) Ecological modernization: new perspectives. Journal of Cleaner Production, 16: 557-65.

Jänicke, M., Mönch, H. and Binder, M. (2000) Structural change and environmental policy. In S. Young (ed.) The Emergence of Ecological Modernization: Integrating the Environment and the Economy? London: Routledge.

Jenkins, R. (2001) Corporate Codes of Conduct—Self-regulation in a Global Economy. Geneva: United Nations Research Institute for Social Development, Technology, Business and Society Paper 2.

Kenny, C. and Williams, D. (2001) What do we know about economic growth? Or, why don't we know very much? World Development, 29(1): 1-22.

Kete, N. (1992) The US acid rain allowance trading system. In OECD (ed.) Climate Change: Designing a Tradable Permit System. Paris: OECD.

King, A., Prado, A. and Rivera, J. (2012) Industry self-regulation and environmental protection. In P. Bansal and A. Hoffman (eds.) The Oxford Handbook of Business and the Natural Environment. Oxford: Oxford University Press.

Klassen, R. and Vachon, S. (2012) Greener supply chain management. In P. Bansal and A. Hoffman (eds.) The Oxford Handbook of Business and the Natural Environment. Oxford: Oxford University Press.

Koehler, D. and Spengler, J. (2007) The toxic release inventory: fact or fiction? A case study of the aluminium industry. Journal of Environmental Management, 85(2): 296-307.

Kolk, A. (2008) Sustainability, accountability and corporate governance: exploring multinationals' reporting practices. Business Strategy and the Environment, 17(1): 1-15.

Kollmuss, A., Zink, H. and Polycarp, C. (2008) Making Sense of the Voluntary Carbon Market: A Comparison of Carbon Offset Standards. Frankfurt/Main: WWF Germany.

Konar, S. and Cohen, M. (1997) Information as regulation: the effect of community right to know laws on toxic emissions. Journal of Environmental Economics and Management, 32: 100-24.

Korhonen, J. (2002) Two paths to industrial ecology: applying the product-based and geographical approaches. Journal of Environmental Planning and Management, 45(1): 39-57.

Kossoy, K. and Ambrosi, P. (2010) The state and trends of the carbon market. Washington, DC: Environment Department, World Bank.

Kruger, J. (2005) From SO_2 to greenhouse gases trends and events shaping future emissions trading programs in the United States. Resources for the Future Discussion Paper 05-20. Washington, DC: Resources for the Future.

Krut, R. and Gleckman, H. (1998) ISO 14000: A Missed Opportunity for Sustainable Global Development. London: Earthscan Publications.

Kysar, D. and Meyler, B. (2008) Like a nation state. UCLA Law Review, 55(6): 1621-73.

Laasch, O. and Conaway, R. (2015) Principles of Responsible Management. Global Sustainability, Responsibility, and Ethics. Stamford, CT: Cengage.

Labatt, S. and Maclaren, V.W. (1998) Voluntary corporate environmental initiatives: a typology and preliminary investigation. Environment and Planning C, 16: 191-209.

Landry, M., Siems, A., Stedge, G. and Abt Associates (2005) Applying lessons learned from wetlands mitigation banking to water quality trading. Report for Office of Policy, Economics and Innovation and Office of Water. Washington, DC: Environmental Protection Agency.

Laszlo, C. and Zhexembayeva, N. (2011) Embedded Sustainability—The Next Big Competitive Advantage. Sheffield: Greenleaf.

Lehmann, S. and Crocker, R. (eds.) (2012) Designing for Zero Waste: Consumption, Technologies and the Built Environment. London: Earthscan.

Lenox, M. and Nash, J. (2003) Industry self-regulation and adverse selection: a comparison of four trade association programs. Business Strategy and the Environment, 12: 343-56.

Lindhqvist, T. (2000) Extended producer responsibility in cleaner production policy principle to promote environmental improvements of product systems. Doctoral dissertation, Lund University.

Lynn, F. and Kartez, J. (1997) Environmental democracy in action: the political economy of corporate environmentalism. Journal of Law and Economics, XLIII(October): 583-617.

McDonough, W. and Braungart, M. (2002) Cradle to Cradle: Remaking the Way We Make Things. New York: North Point Press.

Mitchell, C. and Woodman, B. (2010) Regulation and sustainable energy systems. In R. Baldwin, M. Cave and M. Lodge (eds.) The Oxford Handbook of Regulation. Oxford Handbooks Online: www.oxfordhandbooks.com

Morad, M. (2007) An exploratory review of the role of ecological modernisation in supporting local economies green drive. Local Economy, 22(1): 27-39.

Morgan, K. (2010) Local and green, global and fair: the ethical foodscape and the politics of care. Environment and Planning A, 42: 1852-67.

Moscardo, G. (2013) Marketing and sustainability. In G. Mascardo, G. Lamberton, G. Wells et al. (eds.) Sustainability in Australian Business: Principles and Practice. Milton, QLD: John Wiley & Sons.

Murphy, J. and Gouldson, A. (2000) Environmental policy and industrial innovation: integrating environment and economy through ecological modernization. Geoforum, 31: 33-44.

Nadaï, A. (1999) Conditions for the development of a product ecolabel. European Environment, 9: 202-11.

Nemetz, P. (2013), Business and Sustainability Challenge: An Integrated Perspective. New York: Routledge.

New Zealand Productivity Commission (2014) Regulatory Institutions and Practices. Wellington: New Zealand Productivity Commission. Online at: www .productivity.govt.nz

Organisation for Economic Cooperation and Development (OECD) (1994) Applying Economic Instruments to Environmental Policies in OECD and Dynamic Non-member Countries. Paris: OECD.

Organisation for Economic Cooperation and Development (OECD) (1995) Recommendations of the Council of the OECD on Improving the Regulatory Quality and Performance. Paris: OECD.

Organisation for Economic Cooperation and Development (OECD) (1996) Environmental Performance Review: New Zealand. Paris: OECD.

Organisation for Economic Cooperation and Development (OECD) (2007) OECD Environmental Performance Reviews New Zealand. Paris: OECD.

Organisation for Economic Cooperation and Development (OECD) (2010) OECD Interim Report of the Green Growth Strategy: Implementing our Commitment for a Sustainable Future. Meeting of the OECD Council at Ministerial Level. Paris: OECD.

Organisation for Economic Cooperation and Development (OECD) (2011) Towards Green Growth: Monitoring Progress. Paris: OECD.

Oldenburg, K. and Geiser, K. (1997) Pollution prevention and/or industrial ecology? Journal of Cleaner Production, 5(1-2): 103-8.

Olson, M. (1971) The Logic of Collective Action: Public Goods and the Theory of Groups. Cambridge, MA: Harvard University Press.

O'Rourke, A. (2003) The message and the methods of ethical investment. Journal of Cleaner Production, 11(6): 464-80.

Pargal, S. and Wheeler, D. (1996) Informal regulation of industrial pollution in developing countries: evidence from Indonesia. Journal of Political Economy, 104: 1314-27.

Parry, I. (2002) Are Tradable Permits a Good Idea? Resources for the Future Issues Brief 02-33. Washington, DC: Resources for the Future.

Pawson, R. and Tilley, N. (1997) Realistic Evaluation. London: Sage.

Pearce, D. and Warford, J. (1993) World Without End. New York: Oxford University Press.

Perrow, C. (1984) Normal Accidents: Living with High-Risk Technologies. Princeton, NJ: Princeton University Press.

Perrow, C. (2007) The Next Catastrophe: Reducing Our Vulnerabilities to Natural, Industrial, and Terrorist Disasters. Princeton, NJ: Princeton University Press.

Perry, M. (2009) Trade associations: exploring the Trans-Tasman environment for business associability. Journal of Management & Organization, 154: 404-22.

Perry, M. (2010) Controversies in Local Economic Development. Abington: Routledge.

Perry, M. (2014) Luxury Lodges New Zealand and prospects for elegant disruption. In M. Gardetti and A. Torres (eds.) Sustainable Luxury: Managing Social and Environmental Performance in Iconic Brands. Sheffield: Greenleaf.

Perry, M. and Battisti, M. (2011) Sustainable business and local economic development. In G. Eweje and M. Perry (eds.) Business and Sustainability: Concepts, Strategies and Changes. Critical Studies on Corporate Responsibility, Governance and Sustainability, Volume 3. Bradford: Emerald.

Petts, J. (2000) The regulator-regulated relationship and environmental protection: perceptions in small and medium-sized enterprises. Environment and Planning A, 18: 191-206.

Petts, J., Herd, A., Gerrard, S. and Horne, C. (1999) The climate and culture of environmental compliance within SMEs. Business Strategy and the Environment, 8: 14-30.

Porter, M. and Kramer, M. (2006) Strategy & society: the link between competitive advantage and corporate responsibility. Harvard Business Review, December: 1-17.

Porter, M. and Kramer, M. (2011) Creating shared value. Harvard Business Review, January–February: 1-17.

Porter, M. and van der Linde, C. (1995) Green and competitive: ending the stalemate. Harvard Business Review, September: 120—9.

Rainey, D. (2005) Sustainable Business Development. Cambridge: Cambridge University Press.

Roberts, J. (2011) Environmental Policy. Abington: Routledge.

Robson, C. (2002) Real World Research, 2nd edition. London: Routledge.

Rumsfeld, D. (2002) News conference transcript, February 12. Online at: http://www.defense.gov/Transcripts/Transcripts.aspx?TranscriptID=2636

Salzmann, O., Ionescu-Somers, A. and Steger, U. (2005) The business case for corporate sustainability: literature review and research options. European Management Journal, 23(1): 27-36.

Schmalensee, R. and Stavins, R. (2012) The SO_2 allowance trading system: the ironic history of a grand policy experiment. Resources for the Future Discussion Paper 12-44.Washington DC: Resources for the Future.

Scholtz, J. (1984) Cooperation, deterrence, and the ecology of regulatory enforcement. Law & Society Review, 18: 179-224.

Smit, A., Driessen, P. and Glasbergen, P. (2008) Constraints on the conversion to sustainable production: the case of the Dutch potato chain. Business Strategy and the Environment, 17(6): 369-81.

Sterner, T. (2003) Policy Instruments for Environmental and Natural Resource Management. Washington, DC: Resources for the Future.

Stavins, R. (2003) Market-based environmental policies: what can we learn from US experience (and related research)? Resources for the Future Discussion Paper 03-43. Washington, DC: Resources for the Future.

Steger, U. (2004) The Business of Sustainability: Building Industry Cases for Corporate Sustainability. Basingstoke: Palgrave Macmillan.

Stephan, M. (2002) Environmental information disclosure programs: they work, but why? Social Science Quarterly, 83(1): 281-98.

Stephan, M., Kraft, M. and Abel, T. (2005) Environmental Information Disclosure and Risk Reduction: Findings from a survey of TRI Facilities, Citizen Activists, and Public Officials. Paper presented at the annual meeting of the Western Political Science Association, Oakland, California, March 17.

Sterner, T. (2003) Policy Instruments for Environmental and Natural Resource Management. Washington, DC: Resources for the Future.

Sterner, T. and Corcia, J. (2012) Policy Instruments for Environmental and Natural Resource Management. New York: Routledge.

Székely, F. and Knirsch, M. (2005) Responsible leadership and corporate social responsibility: metrics for sustainable performance. European Management Journal, 23(6): 628-47.

Tietenberg, T.H. (1998) Disclosure strategies for pollution control. In T. Sterner (ed.) The Market and the Environment. Cheltenham: Edward Elgar.

Tyrrell, P. (2010) Buyers unravel the ethics behind the label. Financial Times, September 15. Online: http://www.ft.com/intl/cms/s/0/13e53632-c0f2-11df-99c4-00144feab49a.html?siteedition=intl#axzz3VQREM

Vachon, S., Halley, A. and Bealieu, M. (2009) Aligning competitive priorities in the supply chain: the impact of upstream and downstream integration. International Journal of Operation & Production Management, 29(4): 322-40.

Vickers, I., James, P., Smallbone, D. and Baldock, R. (2005) Understanding small firm responses to regulation: the case of workplace health and safety. Policy Studies, 26(2): 149-69.

Waddock, S. and Bodwell, C. (2007) Total Responsibility Management: The Manual. Sheffield: Greenleaf.

Walley, N. and Whitehead, B. (1996) It's not easy being green. In R. Welford and R. Starkey (eds.) The Earthscan Reader in Business and the Environment. London: Earthscan.

White, G. (2009) Sustainability Reporting: Managing for Wealth and Corporate Health. New Jersey: Business Expert Press.

World Business Council for Sustainable Development (WBCSD) (2000) Striking the Balance. London: Earthscan.

World Commission on Environment and Development (WCED) (1987) Our Common Future (Australian edition). Melbourne: Oxford University Press.

WBCSD (2006) From Challenge to Opportunity: The Role of Business in Tomorrow's Society. Geneva: World Business Council for Sustainable Development.

Welford, R. (1995) Environmental Strategy and Sustainable Development: The Corporate Challenge for the Twenty First Century. London: Routledge.

West, K. (1995) Ecolabels: the industrialization of environmental standards. The Ecologist, 25(1): 16-20.

Wiener, J. and Rogers, M. (2002) Comparing precaution in the United States and Europe. Journal of Risk Research, 5(4): 317-49.

Wynn, B. (1993) Public uptake of science: a case for institutional reflexivity. Public Understanding of Science, 2(4): 321-37.

Index

This book is a publication in support of the United Nations Principles for Responsible Management Education (PRME), housed in the UN Global Compact Office. The mission of the PRME initiative is to inspire and champion responsible management education, research, and thought leadership globally. Please visit www.unprme.org for more information.

The Principles for Responsible Management Education Book Collection is edited through the Center for Responsible Management Education (CRME), a global facilitator for responsible management education and for the individuals and organizations educating responsible managers. Please visit www.responsiblemanagement.net for more information.

—Oliver Laasch, University of Manchester, Collection Editor

Other Titles Available in This Collection

- *Business Integrity in Practice: Insights from International Case Studies* by Agata Stachowicz-Stanusch and Wolfgang Amann
- *Academic Ethos Management: Building the Foundation for Integrity in Management Education* by Agata Stachowicz-Stanusch
- *Responsible Management: Understanding Human Nature, Ethics, and Sustainability* by Kemi Ogunyemi
- *Fostering Spirituality in the Workplace: A Leader's Guide to Sustainability* by Priscilla Berry
- *A Practical Guide to Educating for Responsibility in Management and Business* by Ross McDonald
- *Educating for Values-Driven Leadership: Giving Voice to Values Across the Curriculum* by Mary Gentile, Editor (with 14 contributing authors)
- *Teaching Anticorruption: Developing a Foundation for Business Integrity* by Agata Stachowicz-Stanusch and Hans Krause Hansen
- *Corporate Social Responsibility: A Strategic Perspective* by David Chandler
- *Responsible Management Accounting and Controlling: A Practical Handbook for Sustainability, Responsibility, and Ethics* by Daniel A. Ette
- *Teaching Ethics Across the Management Curriculum: A Handbook for International Faculty* by Kemi Ogunyemi

Announcing the Business Expert Press Digital Library

Concise e-books business students need for classroom and research

This book can also be purchased in an e-book collection by your library as

- a one-time purchase,
- that is owned forever,
- allows for simultaneous readers,
- has no restrictions on printing, and
- can be downloaded as PDFs from within the library community.

Our digital library collections are a great solution to beat the rising cost of textbooks. E-books can be loaded into their course management systems or onto students' e-book readers.
The **Business Expert Press** digital libraries are very affordable, with no obligation to buy in future years. For more information, please visit www.businessexpertpress.com/librarians. To set up a trial in the United States, please email **sales@businessexpertpress.com**.

CPSIA information can be obtained at www.ICGtesting.com
Printed in the USA
BVOW05s0342090715

407145BV00004B/4/P

9 781606 496701